BRAZIL

TITLES IN THE MODERN NATIONS OF THE WORLD SERIES INCLUDE:

Brazil
Canada
China
Cuba
Egypt
England
Germany
Greece
India
Ireland
Italy
Japan
Kenya
Mexico
Russia
Somalia
South Africa
South Korea
Sweden
The United States

BRAZIL

BY LAUREL CORONA

LUCENT BOOKS
P.O. BOX 289011
SAN DIEGO, CA 92198-9011

Library of Congress Cataloging-in-Publication Data

Corona, Laurel, 1949–
    Brazil / by Laurel Corona.
        p.   cm. — (Modern nations of the world series)
    Includes bibliographical references and index.
    Summary: Examines the land, people, and history of Brazil and
discusses its current state of affairs and place in the world today.
    ISBN 1-56006-621-0 (lib. : alk. paper)
    1. Brazil Juvenile literature.   [1. Brazil.]   I. Title.   II. Series: Modern
nations of the world.
    F2508.5.C66   2000
    981—dc21   99-23478
    COR   CIP

Copyright © 2000 by Lucent Books, Inc.
P.O. Box 289011, San Diego, CA 92198-9011
Printed in the U.S.A.

CONTENTS

INTRODUCTION   6
  The Biggest Little Country on Earth

CHAPTER ONE   10
  Almost a Continent: The Land

CHAPTER TWO   23
  The Colony of Brazil

CHAPTER THREE   37
  The Nineteenth-Century Empire of Brazil

CHAPTER FOUR   51
  The Republic of Brazil

CHAPTER FIVE   65
  Land of Many Colors: The People of Brazil

CHAPTER SIX   80
  The Challenges of Contemporary Brazil

CHAPTER SEVEN   93
  Arts and Entertainment in the Land of Carnaval

  Facts About Brazil   109
  Notes   111
  Glossary   113
  Chronology   114
  Suggestions for Further Reading   117
  Works Consulted   119
  Index   121
  Picture Credits   127
  About the Author   128

INTRODUCTION

THE BIGGEST LITTLE COUNTRY ON EARTH

Brazil is the fifth-largest country in the world, behind only China, Canada, Russia, and the United States. Rivers one thousand miles in length are considered small. The coast is an almost continuous four-thousand-mile beach. One can fly for hours or travel for days in the interior without seeing more than mere traces of human habitation. São Paulo, with 16 million inhabitants, is quite possibly the world's largest city. Itaipú, located on the Paraguay border, is the biggest hydroelectric project in the world. Rio de Janeiro's Carnaval is undoubtedly the grandest street party on the planet.

PROBLEMS AND PARADOXES

The typical Brazilian lives in one of two very different environments, either in a large city or in a small, isolated town. Because Brazil's regions and lifestyles vary so widely, Brazilians have been unable to see themselves as one people involved in a collective destiny; in turn, this inability to unify has led to some of the biggest problems and paradoxes facing Brazil in modern times.

Indigenous people such as the Yanomami live in a world far away from roads and cities. Though lip service is paid to protecting their cultures, when the choice has to be made between preserving their traditional homelands and mining a natural resource or building a new dam, the indigenous people have generally found that their best interests are easily forgotten.

Many mining and other projects are abandoned because the desire for quick profit has blinded investors and planners to serious problems. And even when the projects are deemed successes, the poor rarely benefit. Mining and logging efforts in the Amazon, for instance, have made a few people rich but have left huge scars on the land and few long-term jobs either for indigenous people or for the thousands of workers from other parts of Brazil who came to the area trying to escape starvation. Hydroelectrical projects such as dams, which harness water power to produce electricity, are run by workers whose homes have neither running water nor electricity.

Though Brazil is renowned for its natural beauty, the country's almost limitless size has apparently cheapened that beauty. One stretch after another of rain forest is destroyed because it appears that there will always be more forest. Sewage is dumped into rivers because, presumably, it will wash away. In a poor country like Brazil, it is difficult to choose to preserve natural resources for tomorrow, or spend money on long-range improvements, when people are hungry today.

Brazilians are characterized by a philosophy of living for today and thinking of oneself and one's family and friends above all else. Throughout Brazil's history, neither rich citizens nor poor ones have put much faith in the law or in the government's ability to solve problems, and most Brazilians do not believe that all of life's problems can be fixed. If one has faith, it is in oneself to fashion a *jeito,* a creative quick fix, often in total disregard of the law or of the consequences to those outside one's circle of family and friends.

This ethic of living for oneself and for today is most apparent in large cities such as Rio de Janeiro. The rich residents of Rio live in high-rise beachfront condominiums or behind the fortified walls of mansions in a few choice suburbs. The poor live in hovels crammed against the hillsides. The rich, in pursuit of eternal youth, have made Brazil the cosmetic-surgery capital of the world; meanwhile, the poor have limbs stunted by poor nutrition, rarely see a doctor, and often do not live to see their first birthday. The rich largely ignore the problems of the poor, and the poor, in turn, often resort to violence against the well-to-do residents. Thus, behind the superficial beauty of a city such as Rio is the pervasive ugliness of human misery.

Although the attitude of living for today and for oneself has caused many social and environmental problems, it has also created one of the most vibrant cultures on the earth. Samba music spills out from upscale nightclubs and small dirt-floored taverns. Even the poorest favela, or shantytown, residents dress extravagantly for Carnaval. Brightly painted and tiled homes sparkle in the intense tropical sun. Holidays honoring various saints abound, some offering little more than an excuse for dancing until dawn. Likewise, soccer is a national obsession for rich and poor alike.

Ipanema's modern beachfront high-rises (left) seem worlds apart from Rio de Janeiro's destitute hillside favelas.

This vibrancy is a result of Brazil's ethnic diversity. For hundreds of years, each of the cultures that have made Brazil their home—Africans, Portuguese, Indians, Germans, Japanese, and many others—have been incorporated into something uniquely Brazilian. The faces of Brazilians wear the signs of their multifaceted culture; though not quite the racial democracy it claims to be, Brazil is in many respects farther along that path than are other countries, including the United States.

THE FUTURE THAT NEEDS TO COME

Brazilians joke about their nation, saying it is the land of the future and always will be and a country of never-ending impossibilities. As Brazilians come to understand the depth of the problems facing their nation, pride in their culture has been increasingly mixed with despair and cynicism. But despair and cynicism are also mixed with hope. President Fernando Henrique Cardoso, who was recently elected to a second term, has been extremely effective at addressing economic problems, and it is hoped that he will use his popularity to work on the issues that undermine Brazil's strength as a nation.

In the Pantanal in southwestern Brazil, cows sometimes wander into shallow waters and are attacked by schools of piranha. Within minutes, these large animals are reduced to skeletons by fish that each weigh only a few ounces. As Brazil enters the twenty-first century, this common occurrence could be a metaphor for the swallowing up of this huge nation by the political and social problems that powerful politicians have deemed unworthy of their concern. But then again, it is usually the wounded animal that becomes the piranha's prey, and Brazil has the capacity and the heart to attend to its wounds. It will need to do this if it is ever to become a colossus in more than size.

Ethnic diversity has created a rich, uniquely Brazilian culture.

1

ALMOST A CONTINENT: THE LAND

A map of South America reveals that in addition to Brazil's massive size, the nation is roughly the same shape as the continent as a whole. East to west, it nearly traverses the continent. It stretches equally far north and almost three-quarters of the way to the southern end of the continent. The other South American countries are laid out single-file along its northern and western borders; only two South American countries, Chile and Ecuador, do not share a border with Brazil.

Brazil's size, nearly 3 million square miles total, accounts for the diversity of its geography. It lacks high mountains such as the Andes to its west and the frozen tundra of the southern tip of South America, but nearly all of the other climate zones and topography of the continent are represented in Brazil. It also has some of the most exciting and important cities in the Southern Hemisphere and some of the most awe-inspiring natural and human-made sites.

Brazil is divided into twenty-six states and the Federal District of Brasília, the capital city. These divisions fall into five major regions: the north, northeast, southeast, center-west, and south.

NORTHERN BRAZIL

Northern Brazil is the setting for the Amazon River basin. Although the Nile in Africa is the longest river in the world, the Amazon is indisputably the biggest in volume. The Amazon begins in the Andes of Peru and flows east across the northern end of Brazil for nearly two thousand miles. By the time it reaches the Atlantic Ocean, the force of the water causes twelve-foot tidal waves, and for miles out into the sea, the water remains fresh.

The Amazon River functions as a major route for travel and transportation of goods, but it is as a symbol of wildness and adventure that the river is best known. Along its banks and tributaries live some of the most isolated peoples on the earth. The river is also home to anacondas, piranhas, and innumerable species of butterflies, monkeys, birds, and other animals. Plant life also abounds, including water lily pads large enough to support the weight of an adult human.

But the river is only one of the landmarks of the region. The controversial Trans-Amazon Highway was cut through dense rain forest as a means to facilitate development of the region and connect it with the rest of Brazil. New access to the deep reaches of the Amazon basin has caused outsiders to move in, many of whom have little respect for the ecology or indigenous people of the area. The results have been disastrous for both indigenous people and ecology, although the highway has brought some new trade and work opportunities.

The Amazon basin is an endless expanse of green, punctuated only by rivers, lakes, and the occasional town. Among the approximately fifty towns in the Amazon basin is Acre, the capital of the small state of Acre; and Pôrto Velho, the capital of another small state, Rondônia, both located along the western border of Brazil. Belém, a city with a population of 1 million, is at the mouth of the Amazon and serves as its Atlantic port. The only city deep in the Amazon basin is Manaus, the capital of the state of Amazonas. Manaus is surprisingly large—home to 1.5 million people—considering its location more than one thousand miles from the coast.

Giant water lily pads float along the banks of the Amazon River.

Manaus grew in the late nineteenth century along with the worldwide demand for rubber. It still retains vestiges of its wealth during the rubber boom, including large villas, ornate public buildings, and the Manaus Opera House.

NORTHEASTERN BRAZIL

The continent of South America bulges on its eastern side, coming almost to a point just below the equator. The pointed region is northeastern Brazil. Because it protrudes so far into the Atlantic, this region was the first to be discovered and colonized by the Portuguese in the sixteenth century. The

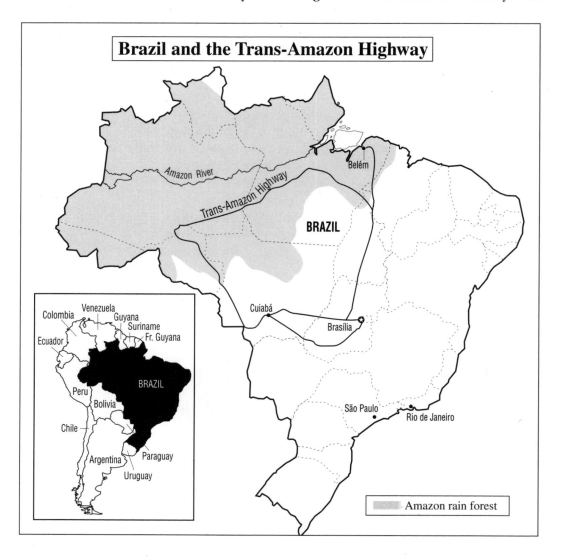

Brazil and the Trans-Amazon Highway

CÂNDIDO RONDON AND RONDÔNIA

The state of Rondônia, located in the southwest corner of the Amazon basin, is named after Cândido Rondon, an army officer charged with putting up telegraph wire in central Brazil and the Amazon basin at the turn of the twentieth century. Rondon sincerely believed in the essential dignity and worth of all human beings, and he came to admire the Indian groups with whom he came in contact during his expeditions. He is famous for his motto, Die if You Must, but Never Kill an Indian, which he expected his soldiers to follow. Because of his attitude toward the Indians, they gradually began to trust him. In 1910 the federal Service for the Protection of the Indians (SPI) came into being largely because of Rondon's efforts to convince the Brazilian government that the Indians needed to be safeguarded. Unfortunately, the efforts of the SPI were not enough, and between 1900 and 1967 almost one hundred Indian groups disappeared forever. Still, Rondon is seen as a hero because he saw a problem and tried to do something about it, and because he showed the Indians the respect they deserved.

In 1981 a small, sparsely populated region in the southwestern corner of the Amazon basin became the newest Brazilian state. It was named Rondônia in Rondon's honor. Unfortunately, the state has honored him in name only. In this area, deforestation and the establishment of new towns and roads has resulted in the removal of Indians from their traditional lands in large numbers. Now, according to David Cleary, one of the authors of *Brazil: The Rough Guide*, "the surviving members of once proud Indian tribes are a common sight huddled together under plastic sheets at the side of the road."

states of Pernambuco, Bahia, and Rio Grande do Norte were wealthy and powerful early in Brazil's history; today, however, perhaps nowhere else in Brazil are the problems greater or more ignored than in these states.

Climatically and geographically, this region has two distinct parts: the coast and the inland region, called the *sertão* by Brazilians. Along the coast some of the most beautiful beaches, charming towns, and delightful cultural life in Brazil can be found. In the drought-ridden *sertão* live some of the poorest people on the earth.

THE NORTHEASTERN COAST

The coast along the bulge of Brazil would fit many people's vision of paradise. The sandy beaches and dunes are lined with palm trees, and the water ranges from bright blue to emerald green. Offshore reefs keep the surf low and perfect for beachgoers. Sunburned café patrons feast on shellfish or the local catch, all of which were probably caught within the last few hours by local fishermen.

City life is entertaining as well. From Fortaleza in the north to Aracaju in the south, the towns are rich in culture and local color. Lace makers, embroiderers, potters, and sculptors sell their work from small shops or stalls. Music spills out from cafés and bars. Local festivals occur weekly in towns located up and down the coast.

Architectural treasures are everywhere. The town of Olinda, a suburb of Recife, is one of several sites in Brazil to be declared a World Cultural Monument by the United Nations Educational, Scientific, and Cultural Organization (UNESCO) for its baroque colonial architecture. Its narrow, hilly streets are lined with brightly painted homes, churches, shops, and restaurants. The interiors of such structures are extravagantly decorated with colonial art. Recife, the capital of Pernambuco, is called "the Venice of Brazil" because of its canals. Recife's most famous building is called the Capela Dourada, or Golden Chapel, because of the large quantities of gold used to decorate its interior. It is one of the most important examples of religious architecture in Brazil.

Of particular note in this region is the state of Bahia. To many Brazilians, Bahia is synonymous with its main city, Salvador—so much so that the city of Salvador is frequently called Bahia. Like much of the northeast, Bahia's culture is strongly influenced by African customs and beliefs, and its population is largely Afro-Brazilian descendants of slaves. Bahia is the center of two of the strongest expressions of this African connection: *capoeira,* an Angolan mix of martial arts and dance; and Candomblé, a religious cult emphasizing trance-induced communication with gods. Salvador is also known for its frequent, colorful religious festivals as well as the opulent colonial architecture in the old part of the city.

THE *SERTÃO*

Travelers who venture one hundred miles inland from the coast soon find a very different side of Brazil. The northeastern *sertão* is a land of misery, subject to long and frequent droughts broken only by occasional floods. Only the valley of the São Francisco River is naturally fertile. People of the *sertão* are usually the first in Brazil to leave their homes when word comes of the possibility to make money elsewhere—whether it is clearing the jungle for the Trans-Amazon Highway, building the city of Brasília, or mining for gold and diamonds in the Mato Grosso. But, according to travel writers Elizabeth Herrington and Richard House, "When the rains return, so do the sertanejos [people of the *sertão*.]"[1] They have their own music, heroes, and traditions, and they are loyal to their region. Today, improvements in irrigation give hope that the *sertão* can be reclaimed for agriculture or grazing.

The Trans-Amazon Highway winds its way through the vast expanses of the Amazon rain forest.

SOUTHEASTERN BRAZIL

The relatively small section of Brazil that makes up the southeast contains its three largest cities: São Paulo, Rio de Janeiro, and Belo Horizonte. Because the states in which these cities are found also produce much of the mineral and agricultural wealth of the entire nation, this region has played a role in Brazil far beyond what its size would suggest.

RIO DE JANEIRO

Rio de Janeiro ranks among the most famous cities in the world because of its incomparable setting and vibrant culture. From one of its mountains, Sugarloaf, visitors have a panoramic view of the city itself, the world-famous mountaintop statue of Christ the Redeemer stretching out his arms, Guanabara Bay, dark green mountains with shantytowns called favelas crawling up their sides, world-famous Ipanema and Copacabana Beaches, and a stunning blue sea. Those who come to Rio during Carnaval, the days immediately preceding the Christian Lent, find themselves in the middle of a frenzied, sensual kaleidoscope of colors, sights, and sounds unequaled anywhere in the world.

These images of the natural beauty of the city and the wild celebration of Carnaval are justifiably famous, but Cariocas,

The famous statue of Christ the Redeemer stands atop Sugarloaf Mountain overlooking Rio and Guanabara Bay.

as the residents of Rio are called, know that the sights, sounds, and activities of daily life are what is really exciting about Rio. The energy of the city is largely focused on entertainment. Nightclubs and restaurants prevail, and the beaches teem with people every day.

Rio de Janeiro is also the name of the state surrounding the city. In the Serra Fluminense, located immediately inland, are two beautiful cities built around summer palaces of the royal family of Brazil: Petrópolis, named for Emperor Pedro I and II; and Teresópolis, named for Pedro II's wife, the Empress Tereza Cristina. Because of the rise in elevation from sea level to 2,750 feet, the temperature in these cities is much cooler, which accounts for their appeal both to the royal family and people today.

São Paulo

With 16 million residents, São Paulo is, along with Tokyo and Mexico City, one of the largest cities in the world. Whereas Rio has a reputation for being all fun, São Paulo has a reputation for being all business. People often comment on the similarities between São Paulo and New York because of São Paulo's skyscrapers, large financial district, museums and art galleries, shopping districts, ethnic neighborhoods, and, unfortunately, huge slums.

São Paulo is also the name of the surrounding state. The fabulous beaches and resorts of Brazil continue along the base of the Serra do Mar, which rises to the plateau on which the city of São Paulo is located. Inland, São Paulo state is an agricultural region where sugarcane and cotton are grown. Of particular note in this region are two small towns, Americana and Santa Barbara d'Oeste, where American supporters of the confederacy came after the Civil War so they could continue growing cotton using slave labor.

Minas Gerais

Located between the states of Bahia and Rio de Janeiro, Minas Gerais, the fifth largest state in Brazil, is the center of diamond, gold, and iron ore mining. *Minas Gerais* means "General Mines," a testimony to the history of this area. The landscape of Minas Gerais is rugged. A narrow coastline rises abruptly to a plateau, which used to be heavily wooded but now is rather bare. The soil is red, evidence of the iron ore still in abundance in the soil.

Minas Gerais has several of Brazil's most interesting cities, a result of the gold and diamond rushes of the eighteenth century. The most famous of these is Ouro Prêto, the former capital of the state. At the height of the gold rush, eighty thousand people lived in Ouro Prêto, more than in New York City at the time. Among these early residents were Jesuit priests who used profits from the mines to build some of the most beautiful churches in Brazil. One of these churches, Nossa Senhora do Pilar, is decorated with 880 pounds of gold dust mixed with paint.

The main city of Minas Gerais is Belo Horizonte, Brazil's first planned city, which replaced Ouro Prêto as the state capital at the beginning of the twentieth century. It is the

A hillside city rises in the state of Minas Gerais, the heart of Brazil's iron ore, gold, and diamond mining operations.

third largest city in Brazil. West of Belo Horizonte, surrounded by iron-red hills on the edge of the northeastern *sertão*, is Diamantina. Diamantina is the center of the second boom in Minas Gerais—diamonds. It houses a museum dedicated to the boom era, but Diamantina is best known as the birthplace of Juscelino Kubitschek, former president of Brazil and founder of Brasília.

CENTER-WEST BRAZIL

The size of Brazil's central western section is astonishing—over 1 million square miles. Its most noted landmarks are a huge floodplain called the Pantanal, the highlands of the Mato Grosso, and the nation's capital city, Brasília.

The Pantanal, located on Brazil's western border with Bolivia, is a region of swamps connected by small rivers that turn into a nearly endless shallow lake during rainy seasons. Roads cannot be built through this almost eighty-thousand-square-mile area. Most travel in this region is by boat or, recently, by small planes. It is a nature lover's wonderland, populated by hundreds of species of birds and fish as well as other animals such as jaguars and wild boars. The main river through the Pantanal is the Araguaia. Known for its clear water and natural riverbank beaches during the dry season, it is believed to contain more species of fish than any other river of any size in the world.

The Pantanal is part of two states: Mato Grosso and the relatively new state of Mato Grosso do Sul. Sparsely populated, these regions are a huge highland plain broken up only by small, low mountain ranges. The name *Mato Grosso,* meaning "thick wood," is a misnomer because only in its northern region, where it borders the southern edge of Amazonas, does it have any woods. The rest of Mato Grosso and Mato Grosso do Sul are dry scrublands.

The only substantial city in Mato Grosso is Cuiabá, which is located almost at the exact center of the continent. Traveling to Cuiabá by railroad and boat used to take weeks; thus,

THE XINGÚ NATIONAL PARK

In an effort to preserve Brazil's indigenous peoples and their cultures, the federal government has set aside lands for them. In 1952 the first such reserve, the Xingú National Park, was established in the northern part of Mato Grosso. Indians can come to Xingú National Park to live in their traditional manner yet benefit from programs such as state-provided health care. It and the Yanomami Indigenous Park in the Amazon basin are the two best known of several such reserves in Brazil.

These efforts have shown some success. The Indian population has rebounded; population counts in the mid-1990s suggest that there may be as many as three hundred thousand pure-blooded Indians, mostly living on reserves, up from an estimated two hundred thousand several decades earlier.

In the 1990s further efforts have been made to demarcate areas for indigenous groups; as lands continue to be taken over by agriculture, settlements, or flooding by the backwaters of newly constructed dams, the task is a daunting one. First, reserves are scarcely a natural environment for those groups who originally lived elsewhere. Second, groups living on reserves are undoubtedly changed from their traditional ways by exposure to the practices of other groups as well as the outside world. Third, these reserves have untapped natural resources such as gold, and it is difficult for the Brazilian government to stop people from taking what is not theirs. It remains to be seen whether the reserves will be enough to keep the indigenous people from disappearing altogether or becoming assimilated to the point where their cultures are completely lost.

the city remained small and isolated until an airport was opened recently. In Mato Grosso do Sul, an area where cattle are far more numerous than people, the main city is Campo Grande. The local population is made up largely of cowboys and Indians, giving it the feel of a city in the American Wild West.

BRASÍLIA AND SURROUNDINGS

The city of Brasília must be ranked among the great all-time achievements in city planning. Recognizing the importance of expanding beyond the thin coastal strip of Brazil, Juscelino Kubitschek, the president of Brazil in the late 1950s, wanted to move the capital from Rio de Janeiro to the nearly uninhabited scrublands of the interior. Today the city and Federal District of Brasília, built from the ground up as an architectural showcase, stand as a monument to his vision, although some argue that its cold modernism, combined with the poverty of many of its residents, make it seem more like a lost dream.

The Federal District of Brasília is surrounded by the relatively small state of Goiás. Northern Goiás has a beautiful green mountain range studded with caves in an area called Terra Ronca and hot springs in Caldas Novas and Rio Quente. These wonders have brought visitors to the region for centuries, as did the discovery of gold in the seventeenth century. Now the springs serve as tourist destinations, complete with luxury hotels and spas.

SOUTHERN BRAZIL

Toward its southern end, Brazil narrows into an appendage comprising the small states of Paraná, Santa Catarina, and Rio Grande do Sul. This is the only region in Brazil outside of the tropics; thus, it is the only region with four identifiable seasons, including occasional snow. It is a region of pine forests and beautiful valleys as well as broad plains, called pampas, on which herds of cattle graze and most of the grain for the nation is grown. It is also a major coffee-growing region.

In Paraná, a narrow coastal strip of beautiful beaches rises sharply to a plateau. Paraná is remarkable for several natural wonders, including Vila Velha State Park, where rocks have

Herds of cattle graze on the pampas of southern Brazil.

been shaped by wind and rain into lifelike forms and mysterious 400-foot-deep holes plunge into the rocky ground. But the most majestic site in Paraná, and perhaps the whole country, is Iguazú Falls, located on the border with Paraguay and Argentina. A total of 275 falls tumble over a cliff nearly two miles long. At the center of the falls is Devil's Throat, where 14 separate falls come together and cascade in a tremendous roar 350 feet to the river below. Nearby is the Itaipú hydroelectric plant, the world's largest. To demonstrate its size, the Brazil National Orchestra gave a concert inside one of the generators while the dam was still under construction.

South of the beautiful beaches of Santa Catarina, the coastline changes and becomes more rugged and rocky with pounding surf. Just inland from the coast is the largest freshwater lagoon in South America, stretching almost one hundred miles. Also inland is Itaimbezinho Canyon, South America's version of the Grand Canyon. It is forty-four-hundred feet deep, four miles long, and over a mile wide in spots, but unlike the Grand Canyon in Arizona, it is green and waterfalls cascade down its cliffs. Farther south, Rio Grande do Sul is famous for its gauchos, the cowboys of the pampas. Pôrto Alegre, with its 1.5 million residents, is the southernmost population center in Brazil.

With a total of 275 waterfalls, Iguazú Falls is a site of unparalleled beauty in the state of Paraná.

From border to border of Brazil, this vast nation is a patchwork not only of beautiful geography and interesting historical spots, but also of cultures. In fact, it might appear that to call something *Brazilian* could mean most anything, but this is not really true. Despite its size, the nation has a history and a culture that, however diverse, is still uniquely Brazilian.

The Colony of
Brazil

In some respects, Brazil's history has been a rather quiet one. No real or mythical ancient cities or kingdoms rose and fell in Brazil. There have been no traumatic revolutions and few heroes or villains of international renown. In some ways, it could be argued, the prime players in much of Brazil's history are not individual people but rather a handful of natural resources. Brazilwood, sugarcane, gold, diamonds, coffee, and rubber all had their turn at the center of events in Brazilian history, and all have left their mark on the Brazil of today.

The Arrival of the Portuguese

Christopher Columbus's landing in the New World in 1492 set off a frenzy of exploration by the seafaring nations of Europe. Six years later the Portuguese explorer Vasco da Gama rounded Cape Horn, the southern tip of South America, and went on to India. Portugal was a small country with relatively few ships and not a great deal of money to finance lengthy sea voyages. However, Portugal was aware that if it did not establish firm control over trade with India, Spain, with its larger fleet and bigger budget for trade expeditions, would end up crowding Portugal out. Portugal promptly sent thirteen ships under the command of Captain Pedro Álvars Cabral on a mission to sail around Cape Horn and establish Portuguese control over trade with India.

Cabral first stepped ashore on the coast of Brazil in 1500. There, he and his crew rested and reprovisioned the ships with the help of friendly Tupí and Guaraní Indians. Cabral sent one ship back to Portugal to tell King Manuel I what he had found, and the rest of the convoy sailed on to India. King Manuel immediately saw the significance of Cabral's discovery: First, it was important to establish a Portuguese presence in the New World so there would be safe harbors for Portuguese ships going to and from India; second, there might be valuable resources in the new land.

"THE LAND OF BRASIL WOOD"

A scouting expedition, sent by the king to draw maps and look for natural resources, noticed local Indians using wood to make a red dye similar to one prized in Europe that the Portuguese called *brasil*. The explorers brought back logs of this wood and subsequently began to call the entire territory Terra do Brasil, meaning "Land of Brasil Wood." This was soon shortened to the word *Brasil*, spelled *Brazil* in English.

In 1500 explorer Pedro Álvars Cabral landed in Brazil, sparking Portuguese interest in the South American nation.

Beyond establishing a firm claim to the land Cabral had surveyed, Portuguese interest in Brazil was not particularly strong early in the sixteenth century. The King of Portugal gave a few grants to individuals to cut brazilwood, but he did not establish permanent colonies. According to historian John A. Crow, "The mirage of India continued to shine, while Brazil was only a country of parrots, monkeys, and dyewood."[2] Other than establishing small outposts that served as stopovers for ships traveling to and from India and as points where brazilwood could be loaded onto homebound ships, no serious thought was given to colonizing the new land.

EARLY COLONISTS

Far from wanting to stay in Brazil, some early Portuguese visitors felt lucky to escape with their lives. Many Indians were interested in the new visitors and provided help and knowledge in exchange for trinkets. However, many had a taste for human flesh. While token cannibalism was practiced by some groups as an important ritual and others might resort to it if necessary, several groups sought human flesh out as a great delicacy. Sailors who became separated from their ships often found themselves the main dish at a very special meal. In fact, the first bishop of Bahia was eaten by the local people.

Despite the deterrent of cannibalism, by the 1530s a few Portuguese had come to Brazil intending to settle. Some were *New Christians,* the term used for recently converted Jews, who were persecuted throughout Europe. Others were *degradados,* people who had been convicted of crimes in

Portugal and sentenced to banishment in Brazil. A few others were Jesuit missionaries who started joining expeditions to Brazil around this time to convert Indians to Christianity.

At this point, the main export was still brazilwood. Demand was so high that French and Dutch explorers began to

---

HAVE YOU NO WOOD IN YOUR OWN COUNTRY?

The Tupí Indians who helped cut and load brazilwood for export found the foreigners' interest in the product incomprehensible. According to historian John A. Crow, writing in *The Epic of Latin America,* one of the Tupí asked, "How is it that you come so far to fetch wood? Have you none for burning in your own country?" The trader replied that there was so much wealth in his country that large amounts of red dye were needed even for a single family. He added that all the wood that had so far been cut had gone to only one merchant. Curious about the apparent greed of that merchant, the Tupí man asked if the merchant was immortal. After telling the Tupí that the merchant was an ordinary mortal, the trader went on to add that, upon the merchant's death, all the money he earned from the wood would go to his children. The Tupí found this incomprehensible, too.

> For why would you endure all the hardships which you tell us of crossing the sea . . . ? The same earth which supports you, would it not support them also? We too have our children and our kin, and we love them, as you see, with an exceeding love, but we know that as this earth supports us, it will in a like manner support them when we are gone, and with this we are contented.

The trader recorded the Indian's words, which represent the intelligence and outlook of the indigenous Brazilians. The wisdom contained in the Tupí's observations seems equally apparent today.

The Portuguese prized brazilwood, which could be used to make red dye and artistic carvings.

encroach on Portuguese territory in Brazil. The continual threat of losing control of Brazil led King João III of Portugal to step up colonization efforts. In addition to protecting Portugal's export monopoly, permanent settlements at key lo-

 ## CARAMARU AND RAMALHO

Shipwrecked sailors like Diogo Alvarez and João Ramalho played a significant role in the early history of Brazil and have left their marks on the Brazil of today. Alvarez was born into the Portuguese nobility but had very little money. He wanted to seek his fortune in the New World, but he was shipwrecked in 1505 along with eight companions near present-day Bahia. Several of his shipmates promptly became dinner for the cannibals who found them, but Alvarez managed to fire off a musket and kill a bird in front of a large group of these cannibals before he could be captured. The Indians named him Caramaru, meaning "Man of Fire," and permitted him to live among them. He spent several years assisting them in battle, and as a sign of their respect, the chieftains offered him their daughters as his wives. One day a French vessel came looking for brazilwood, and Caramaru and his favorite wife sailed with this ship back to France. After loading a vessel for their return voyage, Caramaru wrote a letter to the king of Portugal, quoted by historian John A. Crow in *The Epic of Latin America,* extolling "the delightful province" where his own fate "had been so strangely cast." He returned to Brazil never to leave again. For the next thirty years he was literally the only white in the Bahia area. When Martim Afonso de Sousa dropped anchor nearby, he was astonished to see old Caramaru and a large family of children of mixed Indian and Portuguese appearance. Though Caramaru was useful as an intermediary between the Portuguese and the Indians in the Bahia region, some see his greatest contribution to the history of Brazil as his children, the earliest *mamelucos.*

Caramaru was not alone. In the southern part of Brazil, Sousa found another shipwrecked sailor, João Ramalho, and his large family of mixed Indian and Portuguese children. They were living a few miles inland from the coast, and Sousa decided to take advantage of Ramalho's presence by establishing a Portuguese colony there. To say that Ramalho's little village grew spectacularly would be an understatement; today he is known in Brazilian history as "the Father of São Paulo."

cations would give Portugal bases from which to protect the long stretch of coast it had claimed as its own. In 1532 the king sent naval admiral Martim Afonso de Sousa, along with four hundred settlers and supplies such as seeds and livestock, to establish the first permanent colony at Bahia in the north and another two in the south, near the present-day cities of Santos and São Paulo.

The king knew that Portugal lacked the resources to patrol, defend, and colonize the entire coast, so he established a system of captaincies, whereby the Brazilian coast was divided into sections, each of which seemed to extend inland indefinitely. Twelve Portuguese nobles were named governors of these strips of land. In exchange for whatever profit they could make, they were to pay the out-of-pocket costs of settlement and defense of their region. Though it may have seemed like a good idea, it did not work well. The nobles liked the idea of the prestige, power, and profit they might gain by the arrangement, but they really did not want to be in Brazil, and most were not up to the challenge of governing. By 1549 the king had given up on the nobles and appointed Tomé de Sousa, a renowned soldier, as governor of all of Brazil.

Sousa established a new town, Salvador, on a natural bay roughly midway between the only two captaincies that had actually flourished. One of these was near Santos in the south; the other was in the north in Pernambuco, where colonists had begun to plant sugarcane, the second resource to play a major role in the history of Brazil. Tomé de Sousa's arrival signaled a new era of Portuguese interest in Brazil, and new towns such as São Paulo (founded in 1554) and Rio de Janeiro (founded in 1565) began to spring up. The population of Portuguese colonists grew from only three thousand in 1549 to twenty thousand by 1570.

SUGAR AND SLAVERY

By the mid–sixteenth century, the colonists along the northeastern coast of Brazil had noticed the suitability of the climate and soil to growing sugarcane. Sugar was a scarce commodity in Europe. Sweet foods were considered luxuries, and sugar was as valuable by weight as gold. By the end of the sixteenth century, Brazilian sugar had flooded European markets, expanding national diets (and presumably waistlines) to include desserts and candies. As the taste for sweets grew, Brazil cultivated more acreage of sugar cane and became the biggest sugar producer in the world by 1600.

The huge sugarcane fields in the area around Pernambuco and Bahia caused a continual labor shortage. Indians seemed to be the logical choice to work the fields, from the colonists' perspective at least; the Indians did not agree. Aided by the Jesuit missionaries already in the area, Indians resisted going to work on the sugar plantations. The colonists responded by slaughtering whole villages and forcing captured Indians into slavery. Other Indians died of European diseases such as influenza, measles, and smallpox. As the population of colonists skyrocketed, the Indians were already beginning to be wiped out of northern Brazil.

Indians continued to be captured and enslaved, but by the mid–sixteenth century, the shortage of laborers in the sugarcane fields was so severe that the first Africans were brought as slaves. By the time the slave trade was abolished three hundred years later in 1854, somewhere between 3 and 5 million Africans had come to Brazil as slaves.

PLANTATION LIFE

Plantation life in Brazil was similar to life in the southern states of America before the Civil War. White plantation owners were the aristocracy of the region. Below them were free workers, primarily whites or *mamelucos,* people of mixed heritage. At the bottom of the social order were the slaves, who worked in appalling conditions and often died either from the grueling work itself or from mistreatment by overseers and owners.

Despite mistreatment and the inherent inhumanity of slavery, Brazilian slaves were seen in a slightly different light than American slaves. Historians attribute this to differences between the Portuguese and the English. The Portuguese had had long-standing contact with the Moors of North Africa, and the Portuguese themselves were already more ethnically mixed than most other Europeans. In Portugal, marriage between people of different races did not carry the stigma that it did in England, for example. In the eyes of Portuguese Brazilians, African women were beautiful, and their status as slaves did not make them unsuitable as sexual partners.

Not many white women lived in Brazil at the time. Female orphans were sometimes sent to Brazil to be married off

when they could no longer be kept in orphanages, but the parents of marriageable young women would rarely allow their daughters to go to such a wild and remote place. Only in a few regions did married men bring their wives and families with them. Due in part to the lack of more conventionally acceptable partners, and in part to the generally casual Portuguese attitude toward interracial relationships, unions of white landowners with African women were often open and accepted. Consequently, in Brazil there was substantial and immediate intermingling of African blood with Portuguese. Children of slave mothers and white fathers fairly often were freed, and this free black population contributed from the beginning to the culture and history of Brazil. Ethnic distinctions were quickly blurred or downplayed, and this mingling of ethnic backgrounds in the first Brazilian-born children of Portuguese settlers led, over time, to a culture in which most people are multiracial.

On a Brazilian plantation, African slaves boil vats of sugarcane while a Portuguese overseer (center) looks on.

The *Bandeirantes*

Life for the landowners of the north was quite pleasant, and they had little reason to leave their manors and push inland. They could raise cattle and grow sugarcane near the coast, and the Amazon and *sertão* presented formidable barriers to exploration and expansion of territory. In the south, however, a different culture was evolving. Colonists called *bandeirantes* began to explore inland out of economic need. Forays inland began as soon as the first coastal trading posts were established, but exploration grew in the seventeenth century.

These early explorers, *bandeirantes,* received their name from *bandeira,* the Portuguese word for flag. These "flag bearers" were, according to author Pamela Bloom, "a rugged breed of men, propelled as much by their own personal dreams of glory as by loyalty to the throne."[3] In general, they were groups of poor but ambitious men of all ethnic backgrounds who usually began their journey in São Paulo, following the Tietê River, which was navigable deep into the interior. Once inland they headed farther west, north, or south and often were gone for years. It was largely through the *bandeirantes* that the massive size of present-day Brazil was achieved.

The *bandeirantes* had differing motives for going inland. Many hoped to strike it rich by finding gold and gems, which, although they had not yet been found in Brazil, were known to exist in other parts of South America. Some went in search of Indians to sell into slavery or to convert. According to authors David Cleary, Dilwyn Jenkins, and Oliver Marshall, "None traveled without a priest or two (*bandeirantes* may have been cut-throats, but they were devout Catholic cut-throats), and many bandeiras were backed by the Jesuits and Franciscans in their drive to found missions and baptize the heathen."[4]

Because of the mixed motives within single groups of *bandeirantes,* expeditions rarely went peaceably, and groups often did not stay together for long. According to Cleary, Jenkins, and Marshall, "*Bandeirantes* had to fight Indians, occasionally the Spanish, and also themselves; they were riven with tension between native-born Brazilians and Portuguese, which regularly erupted into fighting."[5] These contentious travel companions often had little to show for their months and years of hardship. Sometimes, to keep from starving, they stopped in the Planalto Central and Mato Grosso to grow crops to feed themselves. Many ended up giving up on their dreams of wealth and settling permanently where their crops had been successful. From these early *bandeirantes* arose many of the inland towns of today's Brazil.

THE DISCOVERY OF GOLD

These early *bandeirantes* brought back stories of great adventures but not much else. This was to change in 1695, when gold was discovered in Minas Gerais. In the ensuing gold rush, large numbers of Brazilians—Portuguese, free blacks, Indians, and *mamelucos*—abandoned their homes

THE CONFEDERACY OF PALMARES

In Pernambuco, particularly during the brief period when the Dutch and the Portuguese were fighting for control, many African slaves took advantage of the chaos to escape into the inland regions of northern Brazil. They settled into a forest existence in communities called *quilombos,* which often replicated the African villages from which they had been taken as slaves. By 1630 nearly ten thousand escaped slaves lived in this area, and they decided to declare themselves a separate republic. They elected a king and named themselves the Confederacy of Palmares (Palms). The population of the area continued to grow, and by the time it reached twenty-five thousand, the colonial government began to think that it was a threat. In 1695 the government hired a notorious *bandeirante* named Domingos Jorge Velho to lead an expedition against Palmares and armed over two thousand slave-gatherers to go into the area with Velho. After months of fighting, the Africans were encircled. Facing certain defeat, they withdrew to the highest mountain stronghold in their region. Starving and sick, several dozen of the last survivors, including their leader, Zumbi, hurled themselves over a cliff to keep from being captured. Today Afro-Brazilian groups who are attempting to rekindle a sense of ethnic pride among Brazil's black citizenry celebrate November 20, believed to be the day of Zumbi's suicide, rather than May 13 as the official holiday commemorating the end of slavery in Brazil.

During the 1600s African slaves formed their own confederacy in northern Brazil.

THE JESUITS

The Catholic missionaries of the Society of Jesus, known as the Jesuits, first came to Brazil in 1549; over the next two centuries, until they were expelled from the country in 1760, the Jesuits became a power second only to the Portuguese crown.

Appalled by the brutal treatment of Indians at the hands of *bandeirantes* seeking to sell them into slavery as well as the colonial government's support of both Indian and African slavery, the Jesuits became active opponents of the slave trade. Beginning around 1600, dozens of Jesuit missions were established, primarily in Rio Grande do Sul and the Amazon basin, both to protect the Indians from *bandeirantes* and to convert them. Well-educated and literate, the Jesuits used their mission outposts as bases from which to defy the colonial government in regard to slavery. One of the best-known Jesuit priests, Father Antonio Vieira, became famous for his impassioned anti-slavery writings and speeches. In one fiery speech, excerpted in *A History of Latin America* by Peter Bakewell, Vieira chastizes parishioners attending a sermon during Lent in 1653. "[D]o you know what God wants of you during this Lent? That you break the chains of injustice and let free those whom you have captive and oppressed. . . . All of you are in mortal sin . . . and all of you are going directly to hell."

But in many ways the missions and the Jesuits failed to protect the Indians. *Bandeirantes* appreciated the ease with which missions could be raided for Indian slaves. Later, when the Portuguese government grew tired of dealing with the Jesuits, who were widely perceived as having established what amounted to an independent state near the Uruguayan border, these well-established mission villages and their Jesuit and Indian inhabitants were easy to locate and destroy. Once resettled into mission communities, the Indians also fell prey to epidemics of diseases against which they had no immunity and to the often cruel tactics of the missionaries themselves. According to Richard House in *Insight Guides: Brazil,* "The Jesuit missions replaced Indian culture with religion and hard labor." The Jesuits showed little respect for indigenous culture and tried, often through force, to get Indians to abandon their customs and adopt European ones. Today the question of whether the Jesuits' overall influence in Brazil was positive or negative is still hotly debated.

Numerous Jesuit missions were established during the 1600s in the lush landscape of Brazil.

and moved to gold country. Brazil was in economic chaos. The great potential wealth of the gold mines was exciting, but the overall economy of Brazil was seriously disrupted. Sugarcane production plummeted as free workers abandoned the fields, and towns that were beginning to thrive in other areas of Brazil went into decline as the youngest and healthiest of their inhabitants headed off to make their fortunes.

In 1719 gold was also discovered near Cuiabá in Mato Grosso, almost twenty-two hundred miles from São Paulo near the border with Bolivia. At the time, the journey to Cuiabá from São Paulo was longer and far more perilous than going to Europe. It took six months and required travel down five different river systems. Along the way, *bandeirantes* were picked off by hostile Indians, drowned in floods, tormented by mosquitoes, and debilitated by tropical heat. In some years not a single *bandeirante* who set out for Cuiabá actually made it.

By 1760 nearly half the world's gold came from Brazil. Adding to the newly found worth of Minas Gerais and Mato Grosso was the discovery of diamonds in 1720 in these regions and in neighboring Goiás. By 1760 gold and diamond fever had reached its height. The Portuguese felt that gold prospecting had increased beyond their control. The people of Minas Gerais and Mato Grosso, with their *bandeirante* background, made rather poor Portuguese subjects. They saw no reason to turn over the customary fifth of their gold to the crown, and smuggling was rampant. Portugal was not about to let the wealth of Brazil's diamonds slip through its fingers. The center of diamond mining, today called Diamantina, was turned into a restricted zone. For many years, people could only come and go if they possessed royal passes.

The gold that the Portuguese government managed to exact as its share of the miners' claims, coupled with its tight control of the diamond mines, maintained Portugal as a world power a while longer. Brazil was Portugal's only real prize, and it had proven unwieldy and unprofitable except for the sugar-producing north. Although Portugal never achieved the same overall status as a world power that its rivals did, it did manage to hang on to Brazil. This was quite a feat considering how badly the recent discoveries of gold and diamonds must have tempted the Spanish and others to

TIRADENTES AND THE INCONFIDENCIA MINEIRA

The gold and diamond boom in Minas Gerais roughly coincided with the American Revolution, and many people in the Minas Gerais area felt they had a great deal in common with the colonists to the north. Portugal, in order to get all the profit it could from the mines, had established heavy taxes not only on the gold itself but also on all the goods that miners might buy with it. Portugal forbade local manufacture of goods in order to exact heavy import taxes as well. It instituted countless restrictions on the population, including freedom of passage in and out of the diamond towns.

Some of the better-educated residents of the area began meeting to plot a revolution. They called themselves the Inconfidencia Mineira, or Minas Conspiracy. Their ideas included abolition of slavery, establishment of a university, and construction of factories in addition to the establishment of an independent republic modeled after the United States. They had already chosen a motto to adorn their new national flag: Liberty—Better Late than Never!

Chief among the conspirators was a young army officer named Joaquim José da Silva Xavier. He was nicknamed Tiradentes, or "Tooth Puller," because he also dabbled in dentistry, which in those days consisted primarily of pulling rotten teeth. Tiradentes and the rest of the conspirators were ardent admirers of Thomas Jefferson; they even wrote to him asking for support for their cause, although Jefferson never replied. Tiradentes went so far as to translate the U.S. Constitution into Portuguese and carried a copy with him wherever he went, pulling it from his pocket and reading it to whoever would listen.

The government soon uncovered the conspiracy and arrested Tiradentes and ten others. The trial went on for two years and gave Tiradentes many opportunities to speak publicly about his views. His fame grew, and his ideas became more popular. According to historian John A. Crow in *The Epic of Latin America*, Tiradentes "showed himself to be a lucid and noble spirit whose altruistic motives it was impossible to belittle."

From the beginning, Tiradentes had tried to assume full responsibility for the conspiracy. In the end, the verdict was that only Tiradentes should die for the crime of treason. He was hanged, then quartered, and his head was impaled on a pole as a warning to others. His home was burned and the site scattered with salt as a symbol that nothing would grow from his treachery. Although Brazil was able to become independent without a revolution, it is not true that nothing grew from Tiradentes's efforts. He was the first martyr of Brazilian independence, and his Inconfidencia was followed by others in the growing fervor for independence.

encroach on Brazilian territory. As a result, the development of Brazil over the next century and a half would continue to be influenced primarily by the Portuguese.

THE MOVEMENT SOUTH

A map of Brazil today shows how important the discovery of gold was to the development of Brazil. Most of the major population centers are either in or at the gateway to Minas Gerais and the other more remote gold-producing regions. Rio de Janeiro and São Paulo grew in importance first as stopping points on the way to the gold-rich interior and then as cities in their own right. The capital of Brazil was moved from Salvador to Rio de Janeiro in 1763, a clear indication of the shift in influence. Neither the sugar-growing north nor the new city of Salvador would ever again be thought of as the center of Brazilian life, and both began a decline that is apparent even today.

The gold rush was actually short-lived. By the 1770s the mines were already showing signs of giving out, and only the switch to other activities such as cattle ranching provided a continued economic base for the mining regions of

Young miners work in the gold mines of Minas Gerais. Like the initial gold rush of the 1760s, the 1980s gold rush was also short-lived.

Minas Gerais and Mato Grosso. Still, the gold rush was one of the most important periods in the development of Brazil. It opened up thousands of miles of the interior of Brazil to further exploration and development, stimulated the growth of the first real cities, and attracted nearly half a million new Portuguese immigrants to Brazil in search of fortune.

But Brazil was headed for difficult times. It had more people than ever before, now concentrated in areas that were not well enough developed to support them. It still relied on the heavily criticized institution of slavery. Its mother country was distracted by political problems around the world and at home and was perceived as not caring for Brazil beyond lining its own pockets. Brazilians were not inclined to see their rather heavy-handed Portuguese governors and kings any more favorably than their American neighbors to the north were viewing the British in the late 1700s. Many Brazilians, especially *mamelucos,* already had far more in common with each other than with Portugal, and a strong Brazilian identity was growing. Still, most people thought of themselves as individuals, with real loyalty only to themselves. As the gold dust settled, the future of this South American giant seemed more difficult to predict than ever.

THE NINETEENTH-CENTURY EMPIRE OF BRAZIL

As the nineteenth century dawned, Brazil was both dominated and neglected by Portugal. Its economy was fragile. Its population of 3.5 million residents, more than half of whom were slaves, was scarcely larger than the population of one large American city today. It was a cultural backwater without a single university or even a library. A few Brazilians felt that the way out of their stagnation was revolution, but most hoped only for a little more support and attention from Portugal. They had no idea in what form and how soon that attention would come.

THE PORTUGUESE COURT MOVES TO BRAZIL

Ironically, one of the major figures in Brazilian history was neither Brazilian nor Portuguese. In 1807 Napoléon Bonaparte of France marched his army into Portugal. Prince Regent Dom João, ruling in place of his insane mother, Queen Maria I, knew that if the court remained in Lisbon the monarchy would be overthrown. With cannon fire booming outside the city, the royal family and approximately fifteen thousand nobles and courtiers hurried to the Lisbon docks, where thirty-six ships had been secretly outfitted to sail them to Brazil. The plan was to announce a relocation of the Portuguese court and, hence, the center of the Portuguese Empire, to Brazil. Seemingly overnight, Brazil and Portugal switched places; the mother country became the backwater, and the sleepy provincial town of Rio became the capital of the Portuguese Empire.

This relocation had two almost immediate effects. First, people of wealth and power in Portugal found themselves in an unfamiliar and intolerable situation. They were now what the Brazilian colonists had been—second-class citizens, ignored and neglected by their ruler. Second, Prince Regent

João saw firsthand the negative effect his economic policies were having on Brazil and vowed to improve conditions. He also saw that to live the life to which he was accustomed, he would have to turn Rio de Janeiro into a prosperous, cosmopolitan city.

THE GROWTH OF RIO DE JANEIRO

Simply unloading the ships that had brought him from Lisbon was a step toward establishing Rio as a cultural center. According to historian John A. Crow, "When the . . . royal treasures were taken ashore, Rio de Janeiro at once became one of the best-endowed New World capitals in every branch of the fine arts."[6] João was able to establish a library, an art museum, several colleges, and other cultural centers from the items he brought with him or had sent from Europe. Dom João quickly undertook economic reforms and public works projects, including city sanitation, which would make life in Rio more pleasant. He saw the harm in Portuguese efforts to squeeze undue profit from the gold and diamond mines and the need to diversify the southern Brazilian economy to include more industry and agriculture.

THE RISE OF A BRAZILIAN IDENTITY

Ironically, it seemed that whatever João did to help develop Brazil, Brazilians ended up weakening his hold on the colony. For example, sons of Brazilian landowners were encouraged to go to Portugal to attend universities. Portugal had, quite naturally, been built up in Brazilians' minds as a great seat of cultural, intellectual, and political power. Once there, many Brazilian students came to view Portugal as backward compared to some other European countries. Without Brazilian exports and the tax base of the Brazilian colonies, it was not certain whether Portugal would even be able to remain an independent nation, much less a world trading power. The students returned home convinced that they, as Brazilians, had no reason to feel inferior to the Portuguese, and they were ready to use their educations to promote Brazilian independence.

After Napoléon's final defeat at Waterloo in 1815, many Brazilians assumed that their days as the capital of the Portuguese Empire would soon be over. João, they figured, would soon be taking the court back to Lisbon. But João had come to prefer life among Brazilians, and he was in no hurry to return to the backbiting arrogance of the Portuguese court. He also watched anxiously as the number of conspiracies and small uprisings against the monarchy grew in Brazil, and incursions onto Brazilian territory by other European powers such as France became more frequent. João, who had become King John VI of Portugal and Brazil in 1816, was concerned that if he returned to Lisbon the Portuguese colony of Brazil might be conquered by outsiders or declared an independent nation by Brazilians. Despite growing antipathy toward the monarchy, João stayed a few more years, founding the first newspaper, bank, military academies, medical school, theater, and observatory—and secretly looting the national treasury for his own personal use. Finally his absence became too much for the government in Lisbon, and João realized he might lose power in Portugal as well as in

AT SEA WITH THE ROYAL COURT

After the port of Lisbon had faded into the horizon, and they were safely beyond the reach of Napoléon's guns, the reality of the situation facing the fleeing Portuguese court quickly became apparent. Although they had managed to load supplies of water and perishable food aboard the ships, they were not nearly enough, especially for people who were not used to deprivation. The situation was made worse by the fact that the ships were seriously overcrowded with people who decided to come along at the last minute. Then it was discovered that, in the rush to escape, all of the clothes for most of the court had been left on the docks. For the entire duration of the voyage, people would be unable to change clothes. Indigestion, seasickness, perspiration, and other bodily functions soon made the stench of the living quarters nearly unbearable. The queen got lice in her hair and had to be shaved bald.

The crossing was a long and stormy one, taking almost two months. By the time the ships arrived in Bahia, the passengers were in terrible shape. They were too embarrassed to come ashore because their appearance was decidedly undignified. Every home in Bahia was searched for donations of clothing, and the finest pieces were willingly turned over to the royal entourage. The Bahians offered the best food they had and helped to bring fresh water aboard. After bathing and a substantial meal, the men and women of the court, many in ill-fitting or decidedly unfashionable clothing, came ashore.

Queen Carlota, who was roundly disliked by nearly everyone in Portugal, got off to a similar start in Brazil. As described in *The Epic of Latin America* by John A. Crow, she announced as she came ashore, "This is no place for civilized people to live." Queen Maria, the demented mother of João, thought she had died when she saw the population that was lining the streets kneel as she passed. According to Crow, she is reported to have shrieked repeatedly at the top of her lungs, "I'm going to hell! I'm going to hell!"

A highly romanticized mural in Lisbon depicts the Portuguese court's voyage to Brazil. In reality, the crossing was brutal.

Brazil unless he returned home. He named his son Pedro, prince regent of Brazil, and in 1821 João sailed back to Portugal. Before he left, he is reputed to have said to Dom Pedro, "If worse comes to worst and Brazil demands independence, proclaim it yourself and put the crown on your own head."[7]

INDEPENDENCE

Upon João's return to Lisbon, the relationship between Portugal and Brazil slipped back into the old pattern of arrogant demands by the mother country and a general patronizing attitude toward its colony. This was not necessarily the fault of King João, though. The Portuguese assembly, or Cortes, like the assemblies of other European countries, was growing increasingly influential while European monarchies were toppling right and left. However, in Brazil, times had changed. A new generation of Brazilians had emerged, at least in the cities of the south, and they were unwilling to be bossed around by a country with which they no longer identified.

Prince Pedro I of Portugal (pictured) became the regent of Brazil after his father, King João, returned to Lisbon.

One of these new Brazilians was a scientist named José Bonifácio de Andrada e Silva who was an adviser to Dom Pedro. Bonifácio encouraged Pedro to resist directives from Portugal that undermined Brazilian autonomy and to develop a broad base of popular support by traveling around the country meeting his subjects. Bonifácio wanted to develop young Pedro's confidence in the idea of parliamentary, or democratic, rule for Brazil so that when Pedro became king he would be more open to the idea of sharing power.

Pedro soon had reason to remember his father's parting words. In a story that is as familiar to Brazilians as Patrick Henry's "give me liberty or give me death" speech is to Americans, Dom Pedro received a new packet of orders from Lisbon while he was resting beside a stream near São Paulo. Jumping to his feet, he ripped the Portuguese colors off his uniform, waved his sword in the air, and shouted, "Independencia ou morte!" These words are known to Brazilians as the cry of Ypiranga, after the name of the stream where he stood when he said them. Pedro was twenty-five years old and had just declared himself king of a brand new country.

JOSÉ BONIFÁCIO

Although Pedro I is famous for his cry of independence at Ypiranga, it is José Bonifácio de Andrada e Silva who is the true architect of Brazilian independence. The year of his birth is uncertain, but it is thought to be around 1763. As a young man Bonifácio studied the natural sciences in France just before the French Revolution. He took from his education not just expertise in his field, mineralogy, but also a revolutionary fervor that he had already connected in his mind with the eventual independence of his own land, Brazil. After a brief and disappointing stint on the faculty at Coimbra, the most prestigious university in Portugal, Bonifácio returned to Brazil. There, he developed a plan for Brazilian independence that would avoid the bloodshed and excesses of the French Revolution and other revolutions in South America. Somehow he would become the confidant and mentor of King João's son Pedro, so that when Pedro became emperor he would chart a course for Brazil that would be to Bonifácio's liking. According to historian John A. Crow, "The regent's character, conditions inside Brazil, the arrogant attitude of Portugal, and José Bonifácio's keen intelligence, all fitted together to make this plan work out perfectly." Later, when the royal court was under pressure to return to Lisbon, Bonifácio convinced Pedro to stay, arguing that he and people like Bonifácio would be able to chart a path of greatness for an independent Brazil. Bonifácio encouraged Pedro to go out among his people to develop their loyalty and love, and it was on one of these missions that Pedro stopped at Ypiranga, where he made the decision to declare independence.

Later José Bonifácio would play a similar role in the early life of Pedro's son. After Pedro I abdicated, Bonifácio became the young Dom Pedro's tutor. By then he was in his late sixties, and he treated Dom Pedro more like a grandson to whom he could impart a love of constitutional government and civil liberty. Once again, through his role as mentor, Bonifácio influenced the future course of his country. He died in 1830, respected as one of the major players in the history of Brazil.

EMPEROR PEDRO I

When a country declares independence, it does not always change its system of government, as the United States did when it replaced the English monarch with an elected president. In Brazil, independence simply meant that the country would have its own monarch and would not be part of the Portuguese Empire. How else it might distinguish itself from Portugal would be up to the new emperor and his advisers to decide. Dom Pedro was crowned Emperor Pedro I on December 1, 1822, and immediately set about establishing Brazil as a constitutional monarchy, a country in which power is shared by both the ruler and the representatives of the people.

Pedro was not a particularly effective or well-liked ruler. He had grown up among servants who catered to his whims and had been pampered perhaps even more than the typical royal-born child because he was subject to frightening epileptic seizures. As an adult he had become self-indulgent, and his behavior had lost him some of the respect he might well have used to be a stronger king. In 1824 a new constitution was drawn up after considerable infighting among the delegates over how much power the king should retain and how much should be turned over to an assembly of elected citizens. Some, including José Bonifácio, wanted a parliamentary-style government elected by the people of Brazil; others wanted a traditional monarchy. Pedro was not a particularly good diplomat, and when he tired of the negotiations, he simply dismissed Bonifácio and other Brazilian leaders and sent them into exile.

Pedro knew he would have to rule with less power than his father had, but he did not know how to do it. According to historian Edwin Taylor, "Pedro was far better at declaring freedom than in defending it."[8] His dismissal and exile of Bonifácio and the opposition lost him a great deal of support, and his leadership was further called into question when a series of mutinies, revolts, and revolutions swept over Brazil and neighboring territories. Brazil lost a significant piece of its western territory when Uruguay successfully declared independence. A revolt in the Pernambuco region of Brazil resulted in the establishment of an independent republic that had to be put down by force. Revolutions were springing up all across South America, such as the one led by

Simon Bolívar in Venezuela. It was becoming apparent to Pedro that monarchs were threatened everywhere on the continent, and weak and unpopular monarchs were the most threatened of all. His support continued to fade, and eventually, under pressure from his deputies, Pedro abdicated the throne in 1831, named his five-year-old son, Pedro, as his successor, and sailed for Portugal.

POLITICS DURING THE REGENCY

Between 1831 and 1840, while Pedro was a child, a succession of three regents ruled on his behalf. It was a time of great turmoil for Brazil. The nation of Brazil was less than a decade old, and it had never really functioned as a constitutional monarchy because of Pedro I's inability to rule effectively. The massive size of the country made a unified Brazil impossible, and its borders were disputed by neighboring countries. Additionally, philosophical disagreements abounded about the practice of slavery in Brazil; as in the United States at the time, Brazil was divided between citizens who found slavery intolerable and those who felt they could not survive economically without it.

The only apparent way to maintain order was to organize Brazil as a loose federation of *patrias*. The *patrias* were fairly autonomous regions with their own governments, held together as a nation by the federal government in Rio de Janeiro, which was responsible for defending the *patrias*, keeping order, settling disputes, and maintaining balance between them. Like the captaincies of an earlier time, this organizational structure was ineffective. A general lawlessness permeated Brazil during the regency period. Discontent among the various factions often erupted into civil disturbances.

Some civil unrest was caused by disagreements about whether to restore Pedro I, continue the regency, or abolish the monarchy altogether. Other rebellions focused on issues of class. Indians rebelled against their near-extermination, blacks rebelled against slavery, and the poor of every color rebelled against the rich. Revolts generally did not spread far from the place they started, and many came and went quickly, often ruthlessly suppressed by the army. There were five uprisings in 1831 and 1832 in Rio alone. Other revolts lasted longer. The Cabanagem Rebellion lasted from 1835 to 1837, and the Farraoupilha (Ragamuffins) Rebellion lasted from 1835 to 1845.

Although Brazil had achieved independence without bloodshed, it could not remain free of violence for long. In fact, by 1840 it was doubtful whether Brazil would survive as a nation at all. Three things happened in the last part of the regency era that preserved the nation of Brazil and, in some respects, set it on the course it has followed since. First, the military grew in strength because of its ability to restore and maintain order. Second, those Brazilians who benefited from the slave economy did not push their own rebellious

THE CABANAGEM REBELLION

The Cabanagem Rebellion was one of many flare-ups of violence that shattered the calm of Brazilian life during the regency of Pedro II. It began in January 1835 in the region around Belém in northeastern Brazil. The *cabanos* for whom the rebellion is named were black, Indian, and mixed-blood residents of cabanas, or huts, on the Amazon floodplain. The hostilities erupted because of the anger of poor people of color against the rich, who were almost exclusively white. Rebels invaded Belém and killed the governor of the region. Sugar mills and factories were destroyed and their owners slaughtered. After several days of bloody street fighting, the *cabanos* were in control of the city and the white population had fled. Rebel bands roamed the countryside, and rural residents were quick to join the ranks of the Cabanagem against their oppressors.

The leaders declared an independent republic in the Belém area, and Eduardo Angelim emerged as their leader, but it was clear that neither Angelim nor anyone else had a real plan for governing. Total lawlessness prevailed. By terrible coincidence, while the rebels were occupying Belém a British ship arrived full of guns and ammunition that had been ordered by the local authorities several months before. The ship was seized, the crew was killed, and the munitions were used to keep the revolt going. In response, the British blockaded the area to try to force the Cabanagem to compensate them for the loss of life and property when the ship was seized. At the same time, the Brazilian army moved into place around Belém, and the rebels were trapped. The rebellion was put down at the cost of many more lives, but eradicating all the pockets of support for the Cabanagem in rural areas took several more years. All told, approximately thirty thousand people died in the Cabanagem Rebellion.

instincts too far. Throughout Brazil, fear was growing that the overall chaos might spark a massive slave rebellion. Third, the elite class rallied around the idea of a strong leader who could help build a sense of national identity and pride. The only person who could fill this role was Dom Pedro. He was not supposed to be crowned until he was eighteen, but it was not clear if Brazil could wait that long. On July 18, 1841, the fifteen-year-old became Pedro II, emperor of Brazil.

THE REIGN OF PEDRO II

If Pedro II had had the personality and childhood experience of his father, his ascent to the throne might have been disastrous, but he did not. During his childhood, Pedro had been shaped into the kind of monarch that Brazil needed. He was serious, intelligent, and self-disciplined. He had been well educated in a broad range of subjects by well-qualified teachers, including José Bonifácio. By the time he was thirty he had gained a reputation as a compassionate, moderate, principled, and astute monarch—and a completely Brazilian one. He had been born in Brazil, an important fact in a country still trying to form a national identity. Pedro projected great personal authority and both scholarly and practical intelligence; Abraham Lincoln once commented that Pedro II of Brazil was the only person he would trust to arbitrate the pre–Civil War conflict between the South and the North.

Emperor Pedro II tried to uphold the constitution and safeguard the interests of Brazil during his nearly fifty-year reign.

Pedro's greatest early achievement was restoring order and peace. He understood what it meant to be a constitutional monarch and neither abused his power nor threw it away. He made good political appointments, choosing intelligent people whether they agreed with him or not, and he exercised what was essentially a supervisory role in the day-to-day workings of the government to ensure that the constitution was followed and the best interests of the whole country remained paramount.

Pedro II reigned for almost fifty years and was widely praised as a monarch. He made a few mistakes, though, that had lasting consequences for Brazil. The first was a series of disastrous military campaigns designed to strengthen and define Brazil's southern border. In 1851 Pedro II sent troops to Uruguay to ensure free trade along and access to the River Plate and its tributaries, a critical trade link for southern Brazil. The objective was not to conquer Uruguay but to overthrow its government. Once successful, Brazil urged Uruguay to join it in attacking Argentina and overthrowing its leader, Juan Miguel de Rosas. By 1853 Brazil had managed to replace the governments of both Uruguay and Argentina with ones that were more friendly to Brazil.

This success emboldened Pedro, but it had disastrous results. An incursion by Paraguay into Uruguay and part of the Mato Grosso expanded into what became known as the War of the Triple Alliance, the bloodiest war in the history of South America. Argentina, Uruguay, and Brazil were allied against the small nation of Paraguay. The apparent superiority of arms held by the three allies convinced Pedro that victory would be swift; however, this was not to be. The war lasted from 1864 to 1870; according to some historians, by the time Paraguay was finally defeated it had lost more than half of its adult male population. Brazil, which contributed most of the alliance's soldiers, incurred heavy losses as well. Pedro was hurt by his military strategy in two different ways. First, it was embarrassing to be so ineffective for so long against a small neighbor, and Pedro's judgment and military leadership were questioned. Second, the war strengthened the army overall, and army leaders emerged as important figures on the national scene.

Likewise, Pedro's reputation was also hurt because he had tolerated slavery when he was morally opposed to it and could have negotiated its end. He did not have the courage to risk losing the support of the plantation owners, so he simply looked the other way during his entire reign. Although the slave trade had been abolished earlier, slavery itself was not abolished in Brazil until 1888, making it the last country in the Western Hemisphere to put an end to it. In fact, Pedro was traveling abroad for an extended period of time and his daughter, Princess Isabel, who was acting as regent, was the one who seized the opportunity. She signed the Golden Law, which abruptly freed the slaves without compensation to their owners, thus throwing Brazil into chaos and incurring exactly the backlash Pedro had feared.

Also, despite Pedro's own love of scholarship, he had not shown an interest in the education of the common people of Brazil. At the time, the ability to vote was tied to literacy. In 1874 only about one in ten Brazilians was eligible to vote. By 1881 the literacy requirements had gotten even stricter, and scarcely more than one in one hundred Brazilians were able to participate in the government through their votes. Political power in Brazil was firmly in the hands of an educated elite that had long favored a republic. They were sure they could rule themselves quite well without a monarch. Pedro's disinterest in public education thereby resulted in a lack of a

Awaiting orders, well-armed Brazilian soldiers line a trench during the bloody War of the Triple Alliance.

During her father's absence, Princess Isabel signed the Golden Law, which freed the slaves but also caused mass chaos in Brazil.

power base for himself among the common people, and he was at the mercy of a small group of people who had grown to resent his power.

THE FALL OF PEDRO II

Losing the respect of the military, and then the support of the plantation owners, spelled the end for the reign of Pedro II. He did not have sufficient backing from any powerful group to put down a military revolt led by Field Marshal Manuel Deodoro da Fonseca on November 15, 1889. Pedro abdicated the throne despite the fact that he was the most popular, and in many ways the best, leader Brazil has ever had. Still loved and admired by many Brazilians, the former emperor was invited to remain in Brazil, but he preferred exile. He died in a Paris hotel room two years later.

After abdicating his throne, Pedro II (left) sailed for Paris, where he would spend the remaining years of his life in exile.

The monarchy was officially over in Brazil, but not because Pedro II had been a bad ruler. It was simply time for a change. Pedro was truly one of the great statesmen of the Western Hemisphere. Historian John A. Crow points out that Pedro "achieved all that could be reasonably expected of a human being. . . . Dom Pedro II was undoubtedly an anomaly among monarchs, but his life was indeed a glowing manifesto of which all Brazilians today are justly proud."[9]

THE REPUBLIC OF BRAZIL

Manuel Deodoro da Fonseca had not intended to overthrow the monarchy in 1889; instead, he had hoped to simply force Emperor Pedro II to replace his cabinet with one more to the military's liking. When Pedro abdicated, the country was caught by surprise, and Fonseca suddenly found himself appointed president of a country with no clear direction or structure.

A NEW CONSTITUTION

The ensuing two years, while a new constitution was being drafted, were chaotic. Factions differed about whether it was better to have a president and federal government with full powers or with extremely limited ones, and they also argued over the role of the military. Eventually a new constitution was ratified in 1891. The constitution established Brazil as a federation of states that would retain most powers for themselves but would be governed by a fairly small central government with an elected president at its head.

The military's responsibility for maintaining order was built into the constitution. However, the military only had to obey presidential orders if they were legal. This was seen as a constitutional safeguard against the president evolving into a dictator, but it potentially enabled the military to act independently against presidents it did not like. Also, active military officers could hold powerful positions in the government. Thus, from the beginning of the republic, the military was allowed to play a large role in Brazilian political life.

THE FIRST PRESIDENTS OF BRAZIL

In the 1891 election, Fonseca was elected president and Floriano Peixoto, another military officer, became vice president. But the chaos of post-Pedro Brazil continued. Brazil had never had a president before, so Fonseca had no models to follow. Also, Fonseca was a military leader and was used to

51

giving orders and making decisions by himself. Annoyed at congressional limits to his power, he simply declared himself dictator of Brazil. Rebellions in the navy and among the civilian elite soon forced Fonseca to resign.

Floriano Peixoto, acting president from 1891 to 1894, was worse than Fonseca. Peixoto quickly earned the nickname "the Iron Marshal" because of the severity of his actions. The navy revolted and sailed into Guanabara Bay in Rio, shelling the coast and setting up a blockade of their own country. Civil war broke out in Rio Grande do Sul and soon spread elsewhere. Peixoto, claiming he was defending the republic, sent in troops to crush dissent. Leaders and suspected sympathizers were executed as a deterrent to others. Peixoto's ruthlessness, combined with the general disorganization of political life, kept him in power until ill health forced him to step down in 1894.

The early years of the old republic set the tone for future Brazilian politics. According to historian Edwin Taylor, "Without exception, from 1889 to the present day, the military have been at the center of every important political

President Getúlio Vargas (center, in dark suit) meets with Brazilian military leaders in 1930. Throughout Brazil's history, the military has been highly influential in the political arena.

development in Brazil."[10] After Peixoto stepped down, a military-backed civilian, Prudente José de Morais Barros, was elected president. The election of Morais brought an end to army and civilian revolts for a time, and it seemed as if Morais was committed to shaping the Brazilian army into a professional force under government authority.

Morais, however, was responsible for one of the worst uses of the military against civilians in Brazilian history. In 1897 he had the mistaken idea that the religious community of Canudos in the *sertão* was plotting a return of the monarchy. He unleashed federal troops on Canudos, which defended itself in a horrendous siege lasting several months. Army casualties totaled nearly half of the nine thousand troops sent in, and Canudos, along with its popular and charismatic leader, Antonio Conselheiro, was eventually wiped from the map.

Canudos spelled the end for Morais. The leadership of the army was unhappy with the way it had been used at Canudos against followers of a man many thought was a saint, and Morais's violent tactics did not sit well with Brazil's civilian population. Morais had to step down in 1898. Over the next three decades, Brazil had a number of presidents of no particular note. At the turn of the twentieth century, politics took a back seat to economics as the natural resources of Brazil again took center stage.

COFFEE

The first of these resources was coffee. The first coffee seedlings were brought by the Portuguese in the eighteenth century. Cultivation was so successful in southern Brazil that by 1850 coffee accounted for nearly half of Brazil's export earnings. Conveniently, the success of the coffee crops came when the gold rush in Minas Gerais was nearing an end and other Caribbean countries were successfully competing with Brazil in the world sugar market. Coffee created a more reliable and long-term substitute to serve as the base of the Brazilian economy at a time when Brazil desperately needed a new export product.

The coffee growers of the coastal south and the cattle ranchers and dairy farmers of the southern interior constituted most of the influential private citizens of Brazil. Their near total monopoly on political and economic power in

A Brazilian port bustles with laborers loading bags of coffee onto ships for export.

Brazil led to the phrase *café com leite,* or "coffee with milk," which symbolized the close links between the two groups. The symbol is even more apt when the Brazilians' sweet tooth is included. Coffee sweetened with milk and sugar accurately sums up the economy of Brazil during this era.

THE RUBBER BOOM

Coffee was not the only product influencing the development of Brazil in the late nineteenth and early twentieth centuries. For a few decades, rubber was equally important. Indians in the Amazon basin had been tapping rubber trees for centuries, using the gummy substance that oozed from the cut trunks of rubber trees to waterproof their boats. One of Columbus's diaries recorded his amazement at a soft rubber ball he saw used as a plaything by Caribbean children.

Rubber was limited in its usefulness because it was so soft, but by the mid–nineteenth century an American named Charles Goodyear had perfected vulcanization, a process to harden rubber. At the time there were 300 million rubber trees spread over nearly 2 million miles of rain forest in the Amazon basin, and the value of this resource seemed beyond measure, especially after the automobile was invented and demand for rubber tires skyrocketed in the United States and Europe.

Rubber briefly turned Manaus, a small town one thousand miles up the Amazon, into the richest and most luxurious city in Brazil. By 1910 rubber was nearly equal to coffee in the amount of money it brought Brazil. The first electric street cars and telephones in Brazil were in Manaus, along with a race course, bull rings, nightclubs, and an opera house. In the middle of the jungle, rubber millionaires sat on the verandas of their huge villas and lit cigars with the Brazilian equivalent of hundred-dollar bills while their wives took baths in imported champagne.

But the rubber millionaires did not know that their good fortune was about to end. Rubber trees grew nowhere else in the world; thus, Brazil controlled the market completely. Although strict measures were taken to keep rubber seeds or plants from being smuggled out of Brazil, it was already too late. Seeds taken from Brazil as early as 1876 by an English botanist had been planted in British colonies in the Far East and had grown sufficiently to be tapped by the end of the nineteenth century. By 1913 the new competition plunged world rubber prices to one-quarter what they had been only three years before, and Manaus quickly sank into decay and decline.

If it were not for the outbreak of World War I, Brazil would have suffered even more than it did from the rubber bust. Instead, demand for coffee, rubber, and sugar grew worldwide because these products were needed for the war effort. The sheer quantities of these products enabled Brazil to make substantial profits; thus, it was able to stop the downward spiral of the economy after the rubber boom ended.

THE RISE TO POWER OF GETÚLIO VARGAS

The 1920s, after the end of World War I, were good times for the coffee growers, ranchers, and plantation owners in Brazil.

THE MANAUS OPERA HOUSE

The Teatro Amazonas, or Manaus Opera House, is one of the most improbable sights in the world. Decorated with white columns, balconies, and friezes, the tall, pinkish-purple building looks like a wedding cake in the middle of a steaming hot and rather grimy city. Construction began in 1881, and the plans got grander and grander until 1896, the height of the rubber boom, when the finished opera house finally opened.

The finest artists were commissioned to paint the ceilings and walls with murals depicting romantic legends about the Amazon. The hand painted curtain by Brazilian artist Crispin do Amaral depicts the meeting of the Río Negro and the Solimões River with the water goddess Yara in the middle. Carved cherubs decorate the corners of the ceilings. Italian crystal chandeliers, seven hundred wrought iron seats, and columns engraved with masks depicting famous artists such as Mozart and Shakespeare were shipped across the Atlantic Ocean and brought by boat twelve hundred miles up the Amazon to decorate the new building. The main architectural feature, a beautiful dome, is decorated with thirty-six thousand tiles imported from France.

The idea of bringing opera to Manaus occurred during the rubber boom, when the city's newly wealthy citizens wanted all the pleasures of life in Europe and were willing to pay unimaginable sums to have luxuries brought to them. However, opera stars did not want to make the journey, and other than an early performance of *La Gioconda*, no full opera was ever staged at Manaus. Famous tenor Enrico Caruso was given an enormous sum of money to come to Manaus, but he arrived during a cholera outbreak and left the city without even getting off his boat. A few famous stars such as Nellie Melba and Jenny Lind gave concerts, the Ballets Russes performed, and plays were sometimes staged, but as a cultural center, and particularly as an opera house, the Teatro Amazonas was a failure.

As a symbol of an interesting chapter in Brazilian history, it is a success. The beautifully restored building reopened in 1996, with an evening of operatic arias sung by José Carreras, and the Manaus Opera House is now a major tourist site.

The majestic Manaus Opera House was originally built during the rubber boom of the late 1800s.

The economy had rebounded and was more stable due to a wider base of products and the continuing strong world market for Brazilian coffee. Since the government was weak, it could not put many limits on the power of the rich landowners of southern Brazil. To the powerful few, it must have seemed that the whole nation was working for their comfort and happiness.

This was soon to change. As often happens after wars, a sense of national pride grew, along with the view that if one fights for one's country, one should have the full benefits of living in it. A younger generation of idealistic Brazilians, primarily military officers and well-educated civilians, wanted to see wealth and power more widely shared. They wanted free education, broader eligibility to vote, recognition of labor unions, and other reforms. Most importantly, they felt that these goals could only be achieved through a strong central government that was able to support reforms, unify the country, and stand up to the wealthy elite.

As usual in Brazil, protests were dealt with mercilessly, which lead to broader and more open revolts. In 1922 a group of eighteen military officers was gunned down on Copacabana Beach when they protested the results of an election. Their deaths started a series of army revolts that eventually overthrew the government. In 1930 the new election produced the same results as always—the election of the candidate favored by the rich and powerful—but this time the army took control and proclaimed as president Getúlio Vargas, the candidate they had supported in the election. The first republic of Brazil had come to an end in the same way it had begun, with the army forcing its will on the nation.

Getúlio Vargas was leader of Brazil for most of the next twenty-five years. He served first as a military-backed president, achieving many of the reforms his supporters wanted: secret ballots, suffrage for women, establishment of labor unions, abolition of child labor, and the institution of a minimum wage. For these accomplishments, Vargas is seen as one of the most significant leaders of twentieth-century Brazil. However, his style of leadership became increasingly dictatorial, and protest was violently suppressed. In 1937 Vargas dissolved the government and proclaimed himself dictator of the *Estado Novo,* or "New State."

During his early career, President Getúlio Vargas worked to improve social conditions, winning him the acclaim of many Brazilians.

Although Vargas's actions earned him comparisons with contemporaries such as Mussolini and Hitler, when World War II broke out he was solidly on the side of the United States and the Allies. Brazilian navy vessels patrolled the South Atlantic, and army units fought alongside U.S. troops when Italy was invaded by the Allies. After the war, returning Brazilians once again demanded a larger role in the economic and political life of their country. Not trusting Vargas's promise of free elections, a group of army officers was able to force him to resign.

Vargas's legacy of social change was such that he remained popular, particularly among working-class Brazilians, and in 1950 he won back the presidency in an open election. His presidency was a disappointment to many, though; it became obvious that his new administration was corrupt. In 1954 Vargas was again pressured by army officers to resign; rather than face the disgrace, he committed suicide in his bedroom in the presidential palace.

A QUICK SUCCESSION OF PRESIDENTS

Brazil had an interim government until 1956, when Juscelino Kubitschek was elected. Under Kubitschek and his Fifty Years' Progress in Five slogan, Brazil entered a period of industrial growth, including the building of electrical power plants, automobile manufacturing plants, and mines. Kubitschek is best known for bringing into reality a new capital city, Brasília, which was built in the middle of an empty plain in Goiás, more than eight hundred miles from the old capital, Rio de Janeiro. Kubitschek believed the way to unify and develop Brazil was to move the seat of government away from the small patch of land in the south, where power had become concentrated, and to bring, in effect, the government to the people. Brasília became the official capital of Brazil in 1960.

When Kubitschek left office in 1961, his legacy included the city of Brasília, the mountain of debt he had incurred to build it, and a skyrocketing inflation rate. The next two presidents were forced to resign without serving out their terms because they were unfairly blamed for money problems Kubitschek had caused. The rich benefited from inflation by investments, but the poor saw the price of food go up almost daily. Economic problems undermined efforts to establish a more democratic Brazil. It seemed that a strong, powerful leader, probably a military-backed one, would be the only way to keep order in the country and set it back on its feet.

From 1961 to 1985, Brazil had seven different presidents, and the military was, in one way or another, behind the rise and fall of each one. None was effective at leading Brazil, and none accomplished anything equivalent to the achievements of Vargas and Kubitschek. By 1985 Brazilians, buffeted by inflation, were tired of mediocre presidents and blamed the military for making poor choices. The military was forced to step aside and let the national electoral college, which indirectly elected all presidents, choose the next president itself.

Under the able guidance of President Juscelino Kubitschek, Brazil enjoyed a period of industrial growth.

CIVILIAN PRESIDENTS

Tancredo Neves, a man with a reputation for honesty, hard work, and independent thinking, was chosen president by the national assembly and was later approved in a national election in 1985. Hopes were high for Neves's presidency when tragedy struck. Neves collapsed the night before his inauguration from a bleeding intestinal tumor and died within a few months from a postsurgical infection. He never took office. Two million Brazilians attended his funeral, the largest public event in Brazil's history.

A stunned nation watched José Sarney, the vice president-elect, become the leader of Brazil. Neves had chosen Sarney as his vice president to calm the worries of critics who considered Neves too liberal. The two men were nothing alike. While Neves was perceived as a man of the people, a brilliant visionary who could lead Brazil into the future, Sarney was seen as a tool of the military, a second-rate political conservative who would keep Brazil mired in the past.

Added to Sarney's problems was the fact that Neves had swept into office with him a number of other ministers and members of congress, none of whom really wanted Sarney to succeed. Sarney was quickly blamed for not putting an end to Brazil's economic problems. According to authors David Cleary, Dilwyn Jenkins, and Oliver Marshall,

> Popular disgust was so great that on every occasion Sarney found himself near a crowd of real people, he was greeted with a shower of bricks and curses. The high hopes of 1985 had evaporated; Sarney had brought the whole notion of civilian politics into disrepute, and achieved the near [impossibility] of making the military look good.[11]

FERNANDO COLLOR DE MELLO

Pressure built for an early election to replace Sarney. This time the electoral college would not choose a candidate and submit the name for the voters' approval, a concept known as "indirect election." Now anyone who wanted to run for president would be able to do so, and the people would choose by "direct election." In 1990 Fernando Collor de Mello, a young, charismatic member of one of Brazil's oldest and richest families, became the new president. Collor quickly tried some

THE BUILDING OF BRASÍLIA

Being president of Brazil during the inauguration of a new capital city was the dream that drove Juscelino Kubitschek's presidency. To accomplish this during the single five-year term allowed by the Brazilian constitution at the time, Kubitschek ordered that construction work continue nearly around the clock from 1957 to 1960. On April 21, 1960, Kubitschek achieved his goal when a grand celebration was held to open the still-unfinished city.

Kubitschek's dream had been assailed by many. The new capital was in the middle of nowhere. Civil servants were not anxious to leave Rio to go work and live away from the cultural center of the nation. Rich and powerful citizens from Rio and nearby were unhappy that their access to those in power would be made more difficult and their property value might drop if their cities declined in importance. Others were concerned about kickbacks and other shaky financial dealings in connection with the construction. Kubitschek knew that it was essential not only to build the city but also to build Brazilians' confidence in it as a symbol of national unity and optimism about the future. He was successful in doing this, and though the concept of the new capital still had its detractors, opposition was not strong enough to stop the project.

The city was praised as a marvel of modern engineering and design. A national contest to design a plan for the city had been won by Lucio Costa. He set the city along two main axes, crossing at right angles in the middle, with one of the axes curved in the shape of an airplane wing. Internationally known architect Oscar Niemeyer, who designed the United Nations building in New York, was chosen to design the main government buildings. Thousands of workers came from the northeast, which was experiencing a long period of drought, and an encampment known as Free City was set up a few miles outside the city to house them.

On inauguration day a mass was celebrated in an uncompleted cathedral, and foreign journalists slept on straw on the floor of unfinished hotels, but no one denied that an astonishing feat—building an entire city—had been accomplished in under four years.

Modern architectural techniques dominate the futuristic design of the Congress Building in Brasília.

LULA AND THE WORKERS' PARTY

When Brazil established direct elections, different groups within Brazil who had felt politically powerless saw that they had a chance to elect candidates sensitive to and supportive of their needs. One such formerly powerless group was the workers of the country. In local elections in 1988, candidates put forward by the new Workers' Party (the PT) won control of several city governments, including São Paulo.

The leader of the Workers' Party was a passionate, articulate man named Luis Inacio da Silva, affectionately known as Lula. He had come to prominence during a metalworkers' union strike in 1980. The strike had been put down by force, but not until it had shut down operations for a month and a half. Lula and several others were arrested for inciting an illegal strike, but the attention they had called to the problems of workers created sufficient interest in forming a national party with Lula at its head. By 1984 the party had grown to include supporters ranging from rural subsistence farmers to intellectuals who sympathized with the problems of the working class.

When presidential elections were held, candidates associated with old-style, money-dominated "politics as usual" were soundly defeated early in the process. Much to the surprise of many, one of the two finalists for president of Brazil was Lula. In the end, the other candidate, Fernando Collor de Mello, won the election by a narrow margin. Many feel that it was a combination of Collor's family name, his youthful good looks, and rather exciting image as a playboy, as well as his incessant painting of Lula as a dangerous pawn of the communist world, that enabled Collor to defeat Lula for the presidency. Though it is impossible to know what would have happened if Lula had won, the corruption and quick fall of Collor led many observers to conclude that Brazil might have been better off under Lula.

Luis Inacio da Silva, leader of the Workers' Party, ran for president in the 1990 election.

drastic measures to get Brazil's inflation under control. These plans included freezing people's bank accounts and borrowing the money from them, promising to give it back within eighteen months. This move did not help the economy after all and angered the middle class, who had helped elect Collor and now felt he had robbed them personally.

Sentiments against Collor skyrocketed when it became clear that members of his administration, his family, and his friends were getting rich while everyone else was expected to sacrifice for their country. Journalists uncovered evidence that billions of dollars of government funds had been siphoned into secret accounts by Collor's treasurer. According to authors Cleary, Jenkins, and Marshall, the scam was "breathtaking even by Brazilian standards."[12] The public, led by students, became angrier as details came out, and Collor was removed from office by impeachment in 1992. Today he lives in luxury in Miami Beach, Florida.

THE LEADERSHIP OF CARDOSO

The presidency was assumed by one of Collor's deputies, but the country's emerging leader was the finance minister, Fernando Henrique Cardoso. An intellectual, scholarly man, Cardoso constructed and implemented a complex program known as the Plano Real, which was successful in bringing inflation under control and stabilizing the economy. This was exactly the kind of leadership Brazil needed, and Cardoso was elected president in 1994.

Over the next four years, Cardoso proved to be an able leader. Cardoso became particularly endeared to Brazil's poor, who had been most affected by the incredible inflation. His skill at building consensus enabled him to avoid losing the support of the major political groups, from wealthy conservatives to socialists. Without resorting to the dictatorial tactics of previous leaders, Cardoso revitalized the economy by privatizing national companies, reducing trade barriers for imported goods, and attracting investment from overseas. Cardoso was also instrumental in developing Mercosul, a South American trading partnership between Argentina, Uruguay, Paraguay, and Brazil. Proof of Brazil's appreciation of Cardoso's effort was the constitutional amendment passed late in his term to enable him to run again in 1998. He won the new term easily.

During his two terms as president, Fernando Henrique Cardoso has been successful in reducing inflation and stabilizing Brazil's faltering economy.

Cardoso has helped Brazil develop a competitive international economy, political stability, and jobs. He has yet to make inroads in reforming the justice system, whose ineffectiveness is seen as fueling violence and corruption. Economic growth needs to be tied to social reforms to narrow the gap between poor and wealthy. Agrarian and environmental reforms are still explosive topics in Brazil that Cardoso will need to deal with if his legacy is to be a great one. Finally, Brazil seems to have found the leader it needs and deserves to bring it into the twenty-first century.

LAND OF MANY COLORS: THE PEOPLE OF BRAZIL

Several years ago two Brazilian babies were switched at birth at the hospital. The ensuing court case to determine custody was covered in minute detail by the news media, except for one fact that apparently was not worth noting: One of the babies was clearly dark skinned and had been taken home by fair-skinned parents, while the other baby was fair skinned and had been taken home by dark-skinned parents. In the United States, although ethnic mixing is more common than it used to be, it is hard to imagine how such clear differences between parents and children would not have been immediately noted. But in Brazil, Brazilians on the whole are so ethnically mixed that any strand of one's heritage, known or otherwise, could easily crop up in one's children.

This mixing of ethnicities is one of the qualities that Brazilians see as defining themselves as a people. While the United States often views diversity as the coexistence of different ethnic groups, each with distinct physical characteristics and sometimes with their own languages, in Brazil the mixing is so thorough that specific ethnic background is often hardly recognizable either in the features of individual Brazilians or in the cultural traditions that are so much a part of Brazilian life. In any group of Brazilians one is likely to see people with a wide range of physical attributes chattering away in their shared native language, oblivious to the fact that in many places around the world their racial differences would be a significant bar to their friendship.

Brazilians boast that they have taken the best of many cultures and transformed it into something different and uniquely Brazilian. When two or more cultures come in contact and produce something distinctively different and new, anthropologists call this syncretism. Brazilian pride in their syncretism is well founded, but to understand Brazil today it is important to go back to the origins of each of the main ethnic groups and to consider their contributions to Brazil's culture.

Brazil's ethnic diversity is showcased during a Carnaval celebration in which Brazilians of Indian, African, Asian, and European descent come together.

THE INDIANS

Although indigenous people may have a less obvious influence on the culture of Brazil than Africans or the various groups of Europeans, their contribution is nevertheless essential to the Brazilian identity. According to writer Joseph A. Page, "The high cheekbones and coppery skin possessed by many Brazilians proclaim the Indian blood that flows in their veins. Indian customs and characteristics have penetrated deeply into Brazilian behavior. Indian myths form a part of the Brazilian subconscious."[13]

The earliest colonists found Indian women astonishingly beautiful and promptly fathered children by them, thus setting in motion the racial blending apparent in contemporary Brazil. Sailors left behind by Cabral and other explorers also learned to appreciate indigenous customs. The Indians believed in a spirit world that affected every aspect of their daily life, and they counted on the *pagé*, or medicine man, to interpret events and cure the sick. According to Page, "Portuguese settlers and their descendants, struggling for survival in a strange, often menacing environment, proved understandably receptive to native beliefs and practices."[14] The cures involved native medicines but also required faith. This emphasis on faith healing was reinforced later by the traditions of the African slaves and is a strong influence in Brazil today. Some sociologists believe that the *Jogo do Bicho,* or "Game of the Animals," a nationwide illegal lottery in which people bet on animals representing numbers, is so popular in part because many Brazilians feel that the spirits of animals can influence destiny.

One immediately noticeable difference between the early colonists and the Indians was their hygiene. Bathing was uncommon in Europe, and body odor was masked by perfume and the heavy clothing. During an Atlantic crossing, personal grooming was nonexistent, and by the time sailors reached Brazil, they must have been very unpleasant company. Left to their own devices, they might have thought one bath would suffice. But the Indians were scrupulously clean, taking river baths more than once a day, and anointing their hair

The attraction that early colonists had for Indian women led to the racial blending that exists in Brazil today.

and bodies with coconut oil. Soon the sailors began to prefer this custom, adopting the Indians' high standard of personal hygiene. Over time, what had seemed a cultural oddity to one generation became the norm for the next one. Today's Brazilians continue what has become a national trait of scrupulous care of their bodies and, especially in wealthy urban and beach areas, physical appearance (now helped along by beauty salons and cosmetic surgeons) is extremely important.

Another trait that some experts believe is tied to the practices of indigenous peoples is the tendency of many Brazilians to move from place to place. Although migrations are often caused by wrenching poverty, one writer has observed that "almost every Brazilian man has at least one itching foot."[15] This willingness to pull up roots to search for new opportunities, and get away from current problems, has been apparent in Brazilian Indians since early efforts to enslave them failed. But the nomadic culture of some of the Brazilian Indians also included agricultural practices that, now adopted on a large scale, have been devastating for Brazil. Indians taught the settlers the slash-and-burn approach to clearing land, and they had what has been called an "extractive" view of the resources of Brazil, meaning that one simply extracts what one needs and moves on. Originally the

Indians taught the settlers the slash-and-burn method of clearing land for agricultural use, a practice that has had disastrous results.

land could support this approach, but it has become a problem in the five hundred years since the first Europeans arrived with quick profit gleaming in their eyes.

Today Brazilians view the surviving Indians among them with mixed feelings. Some see what seems to be a slow passage into extinction with genuine regret and pour their time and money into rebuilding Indian communities. Others consider Indians an inconvenience to the development of the Brazilian economy because their land reserves are known to have precious resources such as gold and even some oil. Others see them as little more than a cultural footnote, a sad but lost cause. Still, no one can deny that they have played an integral role in the shaping of Brazil.

THE AFRICANS

Many colonial landowners had the same attitude about their plantations that the Portuguese government had about its colony as a whole: Anything that did not appear to cause potential harm to their investment was not worth worrying about. Unlike in the United States, where African dances and songs were seen by plantation owners as threatening and were banned even in the slave quarters, in Brazil they were openly enjoyed along with other aspects of African culture.

In keeping with past custom, when the first slaves arrived, many Portuguese landowners on the large sugar plantations of the north simply switched their preferences from Indian to African women, who were also considered very beautiful and exotic. Thus, almost immediately a mixed culture began to evolve.

African slaves were often freed by their masters, particularly if the master had fathered them, and if they were not freed, they had the right by law to purchase their freedom if they had the money. Early in Brazil's history, in addition to the mixed culture of Africans and Portuguese, a substantial free black community began developing its own culture independent of whites. As a result, after a few generations a distinctly Afro-Brazilian culture had evolved.

Music is one of the Africans' greatest contributions to Brazil. The driving beats, intricate polyrhythms, hypnotic vocals, and energetic dances of Africa have infused the musical traditions of every place in the world where Africans were sent as slaves. In Brazil the fast, syncopated beat of the samba, a sound almost synonymous with Brazil, evolved from traditional African music. Brazil's festivals feature a nearly nonstop samba beat combined with lively and sinuous dancing and extravagant costumes reflecting both the Indian and the African traditions of body decoration.

An equally important element of Brazilian culture is the widespread popularity of religious cults. According to Brazil scholar Joseph A. Page, "African deities contribute heavily to, and in turn draw heavily on, an essential element of Brazilianness, a proclivity toward magic and mysticism."[16] West African *orixás*, the name for the gods and goddesses worshipped by Brazilian cults, have been reshaped over time by the influence of Christianity to include characteristics of Mary and other saints. Likewise, African demon figures have blended with the Christian concept of the devil. The two most famous and largest cults in Brazil are directly African inspired and still have African rituals at their core.

The first of these cults is Candomblé, practiced primarily in Bahia, where slaves worked the sugar plantations, and which remains primarily black today. Candomblé was brought to Brazil by the slaves, and today, according to Page, "the rituals are better kept in Brazil than in Africa."[17] A typical Candomblé ceremony begins by a ceremonial ridding of Exu, a demonic figure, followed by a procession of initiates who dance and chant in Yoruba or another West African language to the beat of African drums. Each initiate wears a costume in the colors associated with a particular *orixá*. The main part of the ceremony begins when the *orixás* enter the minds of the participants. This is considered the equivalent of mounting a horse; the *orixás* "ride" the participants, forcing them to shake, convulse, reel around the room, scream, and fall down. At the end, ritual steps are followed to return the *orixás* to the spirit world. Through these ceremonies, Candomblé initiates feel a great release of tension, which leaves them calmer, more focused, and more certain about their lives.

Candomblé requires a serious commitment. To qualify to have an *orixá*, prospective initiates live for several months at a Candomblé house to study the *orixás* so they will understand how to behave when possessed. They also must pay the costs of their initiation ceremony, and because Bahians are poor, this is evidence of the importance of Candomblé

CARNAVAL

It is called the biggest party on the earth. For the four days prior to the start of Lent, Rio de Janeiro and other cities across Brazil explode into a nonstop celebration of the senses. The opening event occurs on Carnaval Friday, when the elected mayor of Rio delivers an oversized key to the city to Rei Momo, the overweight symbol of the excesses of Carnaval. From then on, parties and balls last all night, and the streets are filled with revelers, often in costumes, dancing to street bands, eating and drinking whatever pleases their fancy, and people watching.

But the highlight of every Rio Carnaval is the parade on the last day. The participants are fourteen samba schools who are judged by a government-appointed jury as they march and perform along the parade route. The samba schools are not really schools but rather neighborhood groups, many of them from the favelas, who work year-round to raise money, write and choreograph music, make costumes, and rehearse for their presentation in the parade.

The presentations are dazzling. Each must center around a theme such as a historical event or a legend or occasionally a social issue. The costumes, music, and the signature element of each parade, the floats, must elaborate on the chosen theme. Each school's presentation follows a traditional structure of marchers, dignitaries, dancers, and drummers who assist the entire group in keeping to the rhythm of the school's chosen song. Each entry ends with a giant float presenting, in the form of papier-mâché and styrofoam, the theme of the entry.

There are many critics of the Rio parade. They feel that the event is too far from its roots now, too expensive for the poor people who developed it, too wrapped up in corporate or bank sponsorship, and too touristy. They point

to the fact that in recent years a special venue, the Sambadrome, was built for the parade along a cement corridor into which permanent bleachers have been built, and efforts have been undertaken to have shortened versions of the samba school parade on weekends for tourists. People who remember the earlier Carnaval parades say that the pre-Lent holiday is better celebrated in other cities, particularly in Bahia, where it is not so commercialized. But everyone agrees that the Carnaval in Rio is still one of the major cultural events in the world.

A Brazilian woman dons a sparkling, feathered costume for Rio's Carnaval festivities.

Practitioners of Candomblé, an African religious cult, take part in a candlelit ceremony.

to them. Candomblé practitioners often continue active membership in the local Catholic church as well. In fact, one of the main Candomblé feast days involves a ritual washing of the steps of one of the churches in Salvador. The church shudders at Candomblé, but it has not gone so far as to force cult members to choose between the religions.

One important aspect of Candomblé is the responsibility of the high priestesses to be the oral historians of the community. They are expected to recite accurately family trees tracing all the way back to Africa; thus, Brazilians of African descent are much clearer about their origins than are many African Americans.

The other main African-based cult is Umbanda. It is by far the biggest in Brazil, and some observers argue that it has more practitioners than the Catholic Church. Unlike Candomblé, Umbanda developed in Brazil rather than in Africa, but it is still significantly African in its beliefs and practices. It had its formal beginnings with a Frenchman named Alain Kardec, who, in the 1850s, claimed that it was possible to communicate with the dead and with spirits from other planets. Kardecism was popular in Europe, and when it was introduced in Brazil, it quickly blended with preexisting beliefs and became a new way to summon the spirit world. It appealed to Brazilians who disliked the wild, ecstatic trances of Candomblé but still wanted a direct link to helpful spirits.

Umbanda services are held in a more traditional church-like setting, with altars and benches for participants. The spirits tend to be stereotypes of Brazilian folklore, such as the noble Indian or kindly old slave. Umbanda services have some Candomblé elements but are more restrained; mediums often simply assume an *orixá's* posture, habits, and personality. For instance, the arrival of one *orixá* is signaled when the medium suddenly lights up a cigar. Audience members then come forward to consult about love, work, health, or any personal matter.

IEMANJÁ

Every New Year's Eve, white-clad devotees of the African goddess Iemanjá, who number in the millions in Brazil, go down to the beaches of Rio and place candles and offerings of cosmetic products, mirrors, combs, and other small items on tiny rafts. They wade into the surf and launch the rafts, then shout, "*Muito axê,*" "May you have everything that makes you happy." Throughout December, January, and February, similar rituals are enacted all along the coast of Brazil to placate the goddess, who is considered to be quite vain. Followers of Iemanjá believe that if she is kept happy, the seas will be calm and fruitful for the fisherman and their families. Other followers, who are mostly women, have less direct connections with the sea and may simply respond to Ie-

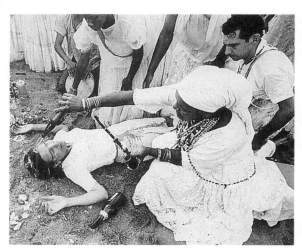

manjá as a female figure along the lines of the Virgin Mary. The cult of Iemanjá is one of the largest within the overall cult of Umbanda, and offerings to Iemanjá are so numerous that some beaches are lined with burned-out candles, soap wrappers, and perfume bottles— the debris left from the offerings.

On a Brazilian beach, devotees of Iemanjá pay tribute to the beloved African goddess of the sea.

Umbanda is a clear fusion of Catholicism with African religious beliefs. For example, Iemanjá, the West African goddess of the sea, is often portrayed similarly to the Virgin Mary, sometimes called by Catholics "the Star of the Sea." The festival day for Iemanjá is one of the most colorful in all of Brazil. Other cults have less obvious connections to Africa, such as followers of Tia Neiva, a now-deceased truck driver who was believed capable of being on several planets simultaneously. Just outside of Brasília, members of this cult gather in the Vale do Amanhecer (Valley of Dawn), which they believe is the center of a cosmic energy field, hoping for interplanetary communication.

Today cult membership cuts across class, gender, color, and educational level. Businessmen, lawyers, and other professionals routinely incorporate cult rituals when making business deals and professional decisions. Politicians often go to cult leaders in search of their support in elections. Whereas cults are seen as oddities in the United States, in Brazil they are an essential part of the national identity.

THE PORTUGUESE

Clearly, the most important Europeans in Brazil's history are the Portuguese. After they brought their ideas about government to Brazil, the country's political history has been characterized by efforts to make Brazil function as a single country under a single leader, according to models familiar in Europe—monarchy, military rule, and various forms of republics.

The Portuguese also brought the Catholic faith, including stories of saints and the idea of church-centered worship. Brazilian churches built during the 1600s and 1700s are among the most beautiful on the continent, and Catholic ideas and practices have remained alive, in part because they have been successfully amended over time to fit the evolving Brazilian culture.

The Portuguese brought European methods of agriculture and introduced new crops that have become central to Brazil's economy. They also brought attitudes about their own superiority and right to take the land they wanted. These attitudes resulted in the destruction of Indian cultures and the enslavement of Africans for hundreds of years.

And then, of course, they brought Brazil its language. It, too, has become distinctly Brazilian. The rhythmic, melodic

The ornate interior of Brazil's San Francisco Church, one of the many Catholic churches built by the Portuguese during the seventeenth and eighteenth centuries.

inflections of African languages have created a variant of Portuguese that differs from the language spoken in Portugal. Additionally, borrowings of words from African, Indian, and other groups have created a specifically Brazilian vocabulary.

OTHER IMMIGRANTS

Early in Brazil's history, efforts by foreigners to take posses-
sion of parts of Brazil were unsuccessful; however, even today
parts of the country show evidence of these early immigrants,
such as the Dutch influence on the city planning and architecture of the coastal northeast. In the southern corner of
Brazil, the Spanish influence is seen in the gaucho culture,
which spills over from Argentina and Uruguay.

In the nineteenth and twentieth centuries, a number of
other immigrant groups came to Brazil in large numbers.
First were the Germans, who began settling in the far south of
Brazil in the early 1800s, and whose influence is clear today in
the timbered chalets of the region. Italians began to arrive in
the first half of the twentieth century as well as a substantial
number of Japanese, Poles, Czechs, and other eastern Europeans; and Lebanese, Syrians, and other Middle Easterners.

THE BLEACHING OF BRAZIL

The racism of Europeans towards nonwhites in the late nineteenth century was apparent in Brazil's immigration policy,
which forbade Africans and almost all Asians from immi-
grating to Brazil but openly encouraged whites. This was
done in what sociologists call an effort to "bleach" Brazil—
to increase the number of whites contributing to the gene
pool. Thus, in one of the puzzling anomalies of Brazilian culture, which considers brown- and black-skinned people
beautiful, the loss of a European appearance among a growing number of its citizens was perceived as disastrous.

The success of the efforts to bring European immigrants
to Brazil enriched the culture of the country, but it is difficult to determine its impact on the overall ethnic mix of the
population. When a census is taken, Brazilians are asked to
identify their ethnicity. According to recent figures, those reporting that they are Afro-Brazilian has dropped from approximately 15 percent to under 6 percent in the last few
decades. Brazil's population reporting itself as caucasian has
also dropped from almost 65 percent in 1940 to less than
50 percent currently. Those reporting themselves as Afro-
Brazilians has climbed from 20 to approximately 40 percent
in the same period. Thus, according to writer Tom Murphy,
"Brazil was a black and white nation in 1940, [and] today it
is an increasingly brown one."[18]

LITTLE BAVARIA IN BRAZIL

In the early 1800s Germans were invited to immigrate to Brazil as part of the effort to keep Brazil fair skinned. Most of them found the climate not to their liking, except for the far south, which had distinct seasons and landscapes that seemed more like home. German immigrants flocked to the green valleys and wooded hills of this region, and due to the isolation of the area, they established communities that were in many ways replicas of their towns in Germany. To this day quaint brick and timber houses and town squares complete with German-style beer halls and restaurants abound primarily in the small state of Santa Catarina. The most important of these towns is Blumenau, which has a huge Oktoberfest each fall, second only to Carnaval as a national cultural event.

Originally the isolation of the Germans made learning Portuguese and Brazilian ways unnecessary, and the rest of the country left them alone to continue their traditional ways. Anti-German sentiments escalated, however, during World War II, when Brazil sided with the Allies, and German speakers were viewed with suspicion as spies and Nazi sympathizers. Speaking and learning German in schools was outlawed, and the "Brazilianization" of Santa Catarina began in earnest. After World War II, as roads and mass media have invaded even the most rural parts of Brazil, German is less commonly heard, except in the small towns away from the main centers of tourism and industry, and rarely is it the only language German Brazilians know.

In Pôrto Alegre, a German-style beer hall echoes back to the era of German immigration to Brazil.

Brazil has long prided itself on being a racial democracy, a country where one's color does not influence one's status. Though open racial tension is rare, this myth of racial democracy has been frequently challenged. It is true that anyone who has money and acts correctly will be seen as part of the elite regardless of color, and mixed marriages are common among all groups. Even still, some subtle and not-so-subtle practices reveal a deep-seated belief in black inferiority. For example, job advertisements will require "good appearance." Dark-skinned Brazilians know not to bother applying for such positions. Demographic studies, or even a simple look around the poorest city neighborhoods or most destitute areas of the country, also show quite clearly that poverty wears a darker skin than wealth in Brazil.

THE JAPANESE IN BRAZIL

For many it comes as a surprise that numerous cultural and business leaders of Brazil have names like Onaga, Watanabe, and Yamasaki, or that São Paulo is second only to Honolulu in the number of Japanese residents in a city outside of Japan.

In 1908 approximately 800 Japanese farmers arrived in Brazil as part of what was thought to be only a small, short-term use of Japanese expertise and labor to develop agriculture in the interior of São Paulo state. The Japanese who came to Brazil had been experiencing crop failures and devastating earthquakes in Japan and were not particularly anxious to return home, especially when it became clear that they could do well in Brazil. The original small population swelled to nearly 250,000 by 1950, most of them remaining in agricultural enterprises in the São Paulo and Mato Grosso areas. Those who settled in cities established Japanese communities, the most notable of which is in the Liberdade section of São Paulo. Today there are nearly one hundred businesses and dozens of trades and professional services operating out of Liberdade, serving the ethnic Japanese community and other residents in addition to being a major tourist attraction. One central activity of the Liberdade "Little Tokyo" is a street fair every Sunday where dozens of food stalls serve sushi and other Japanese delicacies as well as arts and crafts. To stimulate local production, strict limitations are placed on imports of Japanese items; thus, traditional Japanese arts such as making kimonos are flourishing in São Paulo while they are actually dying out in parts of Japan.

For several generations, the Japanese largely kept to themselves and did not participate in the ethnic mixing characteristic of Brazil. Recent generations have begun to lose this sense of isolation, and many Japanese are now marrying outside their ethnic group and participating fully in the political and economic life of Brazil.

Indeed, some argue that, ironically, ethnic mixing has blinded wealthier Brazilians to the problems of racism in their country because they do not feel their own background handicaps them socially. To acknowledge that racial discrimination keeps poor people with dark skin on the bottom rungs of Brazilian society would tear at the overall fabric of Brazilian culture. Instead, evidence that links both high social standing and poverty to skin color is discounted by pointing to the many exceptions to the rule. Most Brazilians would agree that poverty is a huge problem in Brazil. However, it is unlikely they will be able to address this issue without abandoning their myth of a racial democracy and coming to grips with the hidden racism that infects their society.

6

THE CHALLENGES OF CONTEMPORARY BRAZIL

Brazil has spent far more of its history as a monarchy and a military dictatorship than it has as a democracy. Powerful Brazilians have not usually put the best interests of the country above their own, and the result has been steadily growing problems that now seem almost insurmountable. In Fernando Henrique Cardoso, Brazil has a president equal to the task, but he leads a country in which people tend to shrug off the idea that problems can be solved through the concentrated efforts of citizens and instead focus on what can be done to make today a little better for themselves, regardless of the long-term consequences.

The favela child knows that today can be made better by tearing a necklace from the throat of a downtown shopper. The downtown shopper has the time to spend shopping because the favela child's mother is her housekeeper. She pays the housekeeper next to nothing, and the housekeeper looks the other way while the child steals because, in the end, it means more food for the family. The businessman husband of the shopper knows that a new necklace will be easy to acquire because today he is lunching with a government official who promises government contracts for his business in return for a small percentage of the profit. The official knows the businessman's products increase the pollution in the city, but that is something to worry about later, and by then he hopes to have enough money to buy a weekend retreat out of the smog and away from the favela children who try to pick his pocket while he is shopping.

Such tangled webs show that it will take more than a *jeito* to solve the huge problems of this huge country. President Cardoso has been credited with reversing the downhill slide of Brazil's economy, but so far he has been unable to address the two problems in Brazil from which all other current problems seem to spring: unequal distribution of wealth and environmental destruction.

WEALTH AND POVERTY

Today, many of the challenges facing Brazil stem from the unequal distribution of wealth. The vast majority of Brazil's citizens are very poor. The cities have huge slums, and in the countryside almost everyone is poor. Poverty has contributed to crime and indifference toward the environment. The wealthy, on the other hand, contribute in their own way to the destruction of Brazil by white-collar crime and indifference toward the less fortunate.

For example, if one looks inland from deluxe apartments in beachfront Rio de Janeiro, across swimming pools and tennis courts, toward the hillside of Rocinha, one takes in at a glance one of the largest social barriers in the world. In Rocinha, shacks climb the hillside; as one goes higher, the level of poverty grows. At the base are shops, churches, and even a bank. Years ago the city acknowledged that the poor were there to stay and provided utilities such as water and

In Brazil's slums, homeless favela children sleep on city sidewalks and resort to stealing to survive.

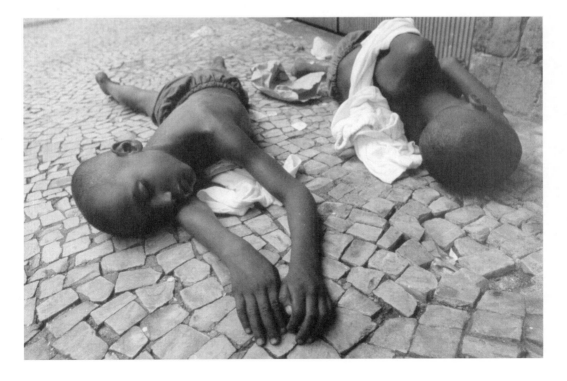

In Rocinha, one of the most destitute regions of Brazil, overcrowding and extreme poverty have led to appalling living conditions.

electricity and graded the streets for vehicular traffic. But the poor kept coming, and the shacks kept rising higher up the hillside. Today only foot traffic can go beyond a certain point in Rocinha, and no utilities or services exist higher up the hillside. The poorer a resident is, the farther uphill he or she has to trudge to get home. At the higher levels, sewage simply runs down the streets, and the stench from human and animal waste and rotting garbage is overpowering. The shacks are so close together that no breezes and very little sunlight ever intrude. Poor nutrition, rat bites, and lack of sanitation all contribute to the ill health of the residents, but they rarely seek medical attention. Police and firemen seldom venture in, and gang violence and fire go hand in hand with sickness as causes of death.

The Rio of the "haves" is worlds apart. It is a world of social clubs, beauty salons, personal servants, cosmetic surgery, fine restaurants, and country homes. Many of Rio's rich rose from immigrant roots through their own efforts and intelligence—a fact they will point to when justifying their indifference toward the fate of others. Part of the problem is that the government is not strong enough to force any sharing of the wealth, nor does it really want to do this. Government corruption is common, and wealthy individuals and government officials often collaborate for mutual gain, getting richer while the poor continue to have nothing. The world of the wealthy revolves around enjoying what one has and making sure there will always be more. The poor are not widely seen as having any rights or dignity; thus, even crimes committed against them by the rich are not taken seriously.

Similar situations exist in all the major cities of Brazil, but poverty is not just an urban problem. In most of rural Brazil, conditions are equally bad. In the northeastern *sertão,* for example, drought regularly pushes people to the edge of starvation. Long-term poverty has many debilitating effects. Professor Nelson Chaves reports that "the population of the Northeast is of low stature, anemic, and, in the sugar zone, is on the way to dwarfism."[19] In the *sertão,* the average woman has between nine and ten pregnancies, and loses half of her children to stillbirth or infant death. The economic growth of the 1970s was fueled by tax incentives to the wealthy to invest in new industries in poor areas of Brazil, but according to Joseph A. Page, "What trickled down to the have-nots was hardly enough to make a meaningful change in the lives of a substantial number of them."[20] Almost all the wealth in the northeast is in the hands of a few landowners and venture capitalists; the rest of the population continues to suffer.

VIOLENCE

Today Brazil is considered a violent country, but it is only in the last few decades that violence has gotten out of control. Experts attribute this to a number of factors. Economic growth has widened the gap between the rich and the poor, and this has led to increased violence. The military governments of the 1980s dealt with rising violence by violence of their own, including the infamous "death squads," which were disavowed but clearly sanctioned by the police. Violence grew not just in the cities but across rural Brazil as well. The end result today is a national culture desensitized to and that almost expects brutality and crime as part of daily life.

Favela residents observe the wealth around them, and because they see no hope of making any significant improvements in their lives within the system, many turn to crime. Roaming packs of children are common in downtown Rio and other cities, robbing tourists and local people alike. Large numbers of these children have been abandoned and form their own street families; others are sent off every day to steal what they can for their families. Drug trafficking, burglary, robbery, kidnapping for ransom, and other criminal activities are daily facts of life in Brazil. In a Gallup poll covering a recent five-year period, over one-third of Brazilians reported that they had been criminally assaulted. Shockingly, approximately 90 percent of Rio de Janeiro's violent crime is drug related and involves minors either as victims or perpetrators.

But the problem of violence is aggravated by the strong-arm tactics of the police and others, and a recent poll indicated that Brazilians fear the police as much as they fear criminals. A 1997 survey indicated that almost half of São Paulo's residents either had experienced police violence themselves or knew someone who had. The criminal justice system is so ineffective that police and others lack confidence that violent acts will be punished. They have come to believe that the only way to get rid of criminals is to kill them on the spot. Vigilante justice is common, and human rights are routinely violated by police officers, who require little pretext to shoot unarmed suspects, including children.

RURAL VIOLENCE

Violence in rural areas is common as well, often linked to land disputes and, more recently, to drug trafficking in certain border regions. Poor Brazilians often move in search of jobs or promises of land to farm. When permanent jobs and land do not materialize, people sometimes settle on land that is not theirs. While nearly 5 million landless Brazilians yearn to own a small patch of land to farm, much of Brazil's farmland lies idle, used as a tax write-off for the wealthy. When haves and have-nots are both armed, violence is inevitable. Amnesty International reported in 1988 that more than 1,000 poor and landless Brazilians had been killed since 1980, mostly over land disputes, and not a single person had ever been convicted. More recently, in 1996, the military police killed 19 landless activists in Pará, prompting President Cardoso to urge congress to make agrarian reform its top priority. Although congress has undercut Cardoso's efforts, other critics blame the president's lack of success on what they see as his insincerity about working on this problem.

Analysts often comment on the irony of the widespread violence in Brazil. Brazilians are among the most cordial, friendly, and easy-going people in the world. Social tensions,

BRASÍLIA TEIMOSA

The magnitude of poverty in Brazil may seem overwhelming, but the story of Brasília Teimosa suggests that there may be ways to make life better for the millions of impoverished favela residents in Brazil. In the 1930s, the government filled in some marshland outside of Recife at the mouth of the Jequía River to build an airport. The project was later abandoned, and soon refugees from one of the many droughts in the *sertão* began building shacks on the land. Their persistence in staying there despite evictions led to the area being called Brasília Teimosa, or "the Capital City of Stubbornness."

By the 1970s as many as thirty thousand people lived there, despite the fact that the area was regularly wiped out in the rainy season by the flood waters of the Jequía, and despite the usual miseries of disease, hunger, unemployment, and early death. With the help of local Catholic priests, the refugees organized an effort to get the government of Recife to install water mains, build a school, and make other improvements that would allow Brasília Teimosa to become a livable, permanent community. After initial resistance, the Recife government was persuaded to divide the land into lots and give the residents title to the land on which they lived. A plan for the community was drawn up, and during the 1980s streets were graded and paved, water systems were put in, and sturdier houses were built.

Today Brasília Teimosa, though still very poor, is a tidy community with a great deal of local pride. Some say its success could not easily be duplicated because it was an example of many factors coming together at the right time. Others point to the fact that leaders saw it as an amusing project or showcase, not as a real commitment to change. But the fact that it worked as a collaborative effort leads many proponents to believe it could happen again all over Brazil if resolving the problems of the favelas were a top priority for politicians and citizenry alike.

Poverty-stricken favela residents find refuge in the Recife community of Brasília Teimosa.

THE DEATH SQUADS

The rise of violence in Brazil is exemplified by the death squads, which came to public attention in the 1970s and continue today. As the urban crime rate rose, the police were unable to keep pace with criminal activity, the courts were unable to try all cases, and the prisons were unable to find room to put new convicts. Frustrated, some police in their off-duty hours began organizing small groups to find and kill known criminals. The authorities looked the other way, even when the victims had been tortured and had the initials E. M. (standing for *esquadrâo da morte,* or "death squad") carved in their flesh, because they, too, saw such activities as being the only way some criminals could be stopped. It soon became clear that whatever rationale there might have been for some of these killings, this new approach to crime had spread beyond ridding the city of its worst of-fenders. Death squads started killing people who owed them money or against whom they had grudges, and they then got involved in drug trafficking and prostitution. The military government denounced the death squads, but it was too late; vigilante killings had become part of urban life.

In 1993, in one of the most horrifying acts of urban violence in recent years, five Rio street children were gunned down execution style as they slept on cardboard mats outside of the well-lit Church of Our Lady of Candelária. Within a few minutes, and only a mile away, three street children in front of the Museum of Modern Art were also killed probably by the same gunmen. The Rio police were immediately suspected.

World outrage about what was called the Candelária Massacre was immediate, and many citizens of Rio were shocked and embarrassed by the heinous crime. But a newspaper poll showed that 16 percent of residents supported the killings, and radio talk shows were flooded by callers who supported getting rid of street children by whatever means necessary. Analogies to vermin are common, and it is clear that poor children are seen by many as little more than rats to be exterminated.

Victims of the infamous Rio death squads lie atop mounds of garbage.

particularly racial ones, seem to be mild, at least on the surface. Brazilians are proud of the fact that they have never had a violent revolution (although they sometimes forget that their history between revolutions has been quite bloody). Still, underneath the surface boils a culture steeped in violence that threatens Brazil's overall stability.

ENVIRONMENTAL DESTRUCTION

Second only to poverty and its resultant violence are the environmental problems facing Brazil. Most notable of these is the destruction of the rain forests of the Amazon and Pantanal, but also significant is the serious pollution and other damage being done by unregulated industry and growth in urban areas.

In the 1970s the Amazon rain forest seemed endless in size. At over 1 million square miles, it was hard to imagine ever being able to make a dent in it. But by the end of a decade of deliberate torching of the rain forest, satellite photographs were showing that one-tenth of it had already been destroyed. In 1988 world awareness of the ecological problems caused by the widespread destruction of the Amazon basin was heightened by the murder of Chico Mendes, a social and environmental activist in northwestern Brazil. Mendes's murder served as a catalyst for international pressure on the government of Brazil to take control of the problem, which seemed a threat to life everywhere on the earth. Brazil has been perceived since then as slow to respond, partly due to the overall political chaos and corruption in Brazil, which has made it difficult to rein in those who profit from destroying the rain forest; and partly because Brazil has so many other pressing problems that it has not been able to make ecological concerns a priority.

Many Brazilians feel that it is not the world's (or even the Brazilian government's) place to tell Brazilians what they can or cannot do. If the best way to feed one's family is to slash and burn rain forests to create clearings to grow crops, it is difficult to argue that the family should starve so that global destruction may be averted in the future. Anti-environmentalists are so powerful that in 1990 they elected as governor of Amazonas a man whose campaign speeches included such lines as "Ten million people can't be condemned to die of hunger

CHICO MENDES

In the past few decades, efforts to modernize Brazil have had some tragic consequences. When the Trans-Amazon Highway was cut through the jungle to open the area to agricultural development and easier trade, the way of life of the indigenous people was disrupted and often destroyed. For centuries Amazonians have made their living fishing, gathering nuts and medicinal plants, subsistence farming, and rubber tapping, but suddenly there were new people with different ideas moving onto the land. Ranchers and farmers, believing that the soil must be good if it supported all that greenery, began moving in and tearing down the rain forest.

In Acre, a state in the southwest region of the Amazon, the forest people began to organize against the intruders. A rubber tapper named Chico Mendes formed a union of rubber tappers whose main form of protest was to blockade areas where the rain forest was being destroyed. Cattle barons and other new landowners were furious at Mendes. They felt they had bought their property fair and square, in what seemed to them to be nearly worthless condition, and now they were being told they would have to leave the land alone. Tension grew between the rubber tappers and the landowners in the 1980s. There were scattered outbreaks of violence between the two groups, and hundreds of people died overall. In December 1988 Mendes became one of the victims. He was gunned down in Acre and became internationally renowned as the first ecological martyr.

Mendes was not against development of the Amazon. His people were poor and could benefit from new jobs and the increased ability to sell their products. What he was alarmed about was how a lack of restraint and long-range thinking was causing the destruction of the rain forest. The international outrage after Mendes's murder forced Brazil to go on record as being committed to finding a way to protect and preserve the Amazon. The development of "extractive reserves," in which indigenous people gather products such as rubber in traditional ways, was one of Mendes's dreams that came true in the aftermath of his death. Both these reserves and the growing international view of the Amazon as a global resource are the living legacy of Chico Mendes.

Rubber tapper Chico Mendes worked to preserve the Amazon rain forest and its pristine environs.

so that animals and trees can grow,"[21] and whose campaign promises included giving every peasant a chain saw.

Complicating the destruction of trees for agricultural use is the fact that rain-forest soil is only fertile for a few years, and vegetation will not easily spring up again where it has been destroyed. When the soil is depleted, subsistence farming families simply move on and clear more forest, leaving devastation behind. Sometimes their slash-and-burn techniques to clear the land get out of control. In March 1998 farmers' fires kindled the worst blaze in the history of the Amazon region and, according to a United Nations representative in Brazil, the worst environmental disaster ever anywhere in the world. More than twenty thousand square miles were burned, an area larger than Belgium.

However, subsistence farmers do only some of the damage. Vast tracts of the rain forest have been destroyed by corporations seeking to extract other riches. For example, some stretches of the rain forest are situated atop iron ore deposits. To build the mines and get to the ore, the surrounding trees must be destroyed. To power the operation, trees must continually be cut for fuel. Similarly, cattle ranchers have destroyed large stretches of the Amazon to create new pastureland for cattle. Others cut the trees for their direct value as lumber. Some stretches have been poisoned with herbicides to assist in the laying of telephone lines and roads. Other parts of the Amazon and Pantanal have been flooded in the backwaters of dams.

Compounding the tragedy of the loss of the rain forest is the fact that many of these projects have been poorly planned and have not yielded the benefit that would have made the loss of some of the rain forest a reasonable trade-off. Two such environmental disasters are the hydroelectric projects at Tucuruí and Balbina. Trees were not cleared before the backwaters of the Tucuruí dam submerged them, resulting in huge losses of revenues from the timber, but more importantly, dissolved chemicals from the decomposition of the trees have corroded the turbines and will probably soon render them useless. At Balbina, the flat surrounding land has spread the backwaters over nine hundred miles of jungle, displacing many indigenous groups and ruining the ecology of the area, but the water volume is so low that it provides little electricity.

Amazon Rain Forest

URBAN POLLUTION

Destruction of the pristine environments of the Amazon and elsewhere are not the only ecological problems facing Brazil; it has a major problem with urban pollution as well. Perhaps the best single example is Guanabara Bay in Rio de Janeiro. The bay used to be an important part of life in the city, attracting bathers, sailors, and fishermen. Today it is as appealing as an unflushed toilet and serves as the receptacle for the untreated sewage from the favelas. Industries along its edges dump other pollutants and toxins into the bay, and now it is a part of Rio everyone tries to avoid.

Air pollution is also a major problem. São Paulo has been particularly affected because of its central role in the economic growth of the 1970s. Manufacturing sprang up all over the São Paulo area, but no planning was done, nor were any regulations put in place to control the environmental impact. The sky grew dark from pollution, but Paulistas, as residents of the city are called, accepted this as a necessary part of the progress that was revitalizing their

INTO THE VALLEY OF DEATH

The São Paulo suburb of Cubatão was once considered the most polluted place on the earth. According to 1980 measurements, ten thousand tons of toxic pollutants were released into the air from factories every day. An additional twenty-six hundred tons of poisonous waste was dumped into adjacent rivers each day, emitting clouds of nauseating stenches and green sludge. The effects on people who lived in Cubatão were obvious. Babies were born without brains or with other serious defects. Half of its residents had some form of lung disease.

In *The Brazilians,* Joseph A. Page points out that "if there was any place on earth where factories should not have been located, it was on these steamy, rain-drenched lowlands tucked against the foot of an escarpment that blocked prevailing winds blowing in from the nearby ocean." But that did not seem to matter in the progress-at-any-cost Brazil of the 1960s and subsequent decades. One minister of planning is on record as having volunteered Brazil as a location for international corporations evicted from other countries because of their pollutants. *The New York Times* reported this minister as saying "Why not? We have a lot left to pollute." Brazil's attitude was not uncommon among developing nations who saw the need to attract foreign investments and industries if they were to improve their economic base.

Little thought was given to the factory workers and their families who would have to live in or near Cubatão and would breathe toxic waste every minute of their lives. Nor was the regular high-tide flooding of the location taken into account. Soon it contaminated the water supply and washed human waste out of the sewers and down the street. Unforeseen was the effect of air pollution on surrounding vegetation. Plant life died on the slopes behind Cubatão, bringing erosion and landslides down into the favelas.

The Brazilian agency charged with protecting the environment has had a great deal of success in the last fifteen years in bringing Cubatão back from the dead. It identified 230 sources of pollution and brought over 200 of them under control. Air and water quality rapidly improved, and today it is better than in some parts of neighboring São Paulo. Vegetation is taking hold, and a few fish are even swimming in the rivers. Children born during the worst years, of course, continue to live with the damage, but there is hope that such tragedies will not befall any more residents of the former "Valley of Death."

Toxic waste flows into a Brazilian river.

city. Soon government reports were showing that the air was so full of sulfur dioxide that it was nearly unbreathable. In 1973 a local artist began appearing in public wearing a gas mask to dramatize the problem. Also, as São Paulo continued to grow, builders either built over or encroached on parks and plazas. The result is what urban planners call a "heat island," where temperatures climb ten or more degrees above what they should be because of the lack of cooling vegetation and reduced air circulation. This leads to a high incidence of heat stroke and intestinal diseases and even isolated flash floods.

The problems caused by the too-rapid industrial growth of São Paulo and other parts of Brazil still need to be addressed. At this point, however, the poor air quality is primarily caused by the more than 4 million automobiles in São Paulo, which lack modern emissions controls and spew more than five thousand tons of carbon monoxide every day. Likewise, sewage treatment is still woefully inadequate, causing one scientist to note that "there is a sanitation bomb around São Paulo, waiting to detonate."[22]

Brazilians have an expression, *para inglés ver,* which means "for the English to see." It has its roots in the nineteenth-century slave trade and early empire and refers to orchestrating things so as to avoid being criticized by outsiders. The expression has rather sly and humorous connotations, implying that Brazilians have their own way of doing things and simply want critics to go away. Unfortunately, this attitude winks at some serious problems that now must be addressed and about which the global community, English and otherwise, has a right to be concerned. Among them are environmental and human rights issues. If history is to view Cardoso as a great leader, then he and those who follow him will need to impact the overall thinking of Brazilians or this beautiful and colorful nation will remain what Brazilians now call it: a land of unlimited impossibilities.

Arts and Entertainment in the Land of Carnaval

In a nation as diverse as Brazil, only a few interests seem to unite everyone. The first is soccer, known as *futebol* in Portuguese. During the World Cup, the business of the nation comes nearly to a halt as everyone gathers around the television or radio. Losses and wins are taken so seriously that the stock market can be briefly affected. Traditional soccer league rivalries, such as that known as Fla-Flu between Rio's Flamengo and Fluminense teams, are played out each year to a backdrop of singing and dancing and even fireworks in the crowded bleachers. Pelé, known worldwide as the king of soccer, is regarded as a national leader and now serves as a cabinet minister. *Telenovelas,* similar to soap operas, are another nationally uniting force, and their stories become more real than the news to many Brazilians.

Despite the overwhelming popularity of soccer and the *telenovelas,* the most distinctive unifying element in Brazilian culture is music. Brazilian music is known throughout the world for its driving, syncopated rhythms, dances, and melodies. Other often overlooked but equally colorful and vibrant parts of Brazil's cultural life are the visual arts—painting, sculpture, and architecture—and literature, all of which have produced numerous world-class artists over the years and continue to do so today.

Music

Brazil's music, past and present, takes nearly endless forms; the fusion of different ethnic elements is what makes it so dynamic and uniquely Brazilian. Indian influence is apparent in some of the percussion instruments, in a frequently nasal style of singing, and in a taste for one-word choruses. Brazilian writer Mário de Andrade also claims that the Indians brought a seriousness of theme to Brazilian music:

PELÉ

No discussion of culture in Brazil could be complete without mention of the biggest cultural icon in Brazil: Edson Arantes do Nascimento, known around the world as Pelé. Pelé, a nickname of unknown origin since childhood, was born in a poor family in Bauru, in São Paulo. He had a contract to play soccer with the Santos soccer club before he had even owned a pair of shoes, and in 1956 he left home at age fifteen to make a name for himself in that city. A physically unimpressive teenager, weighing only 130 pounds and standing only five foot eight, Pelé almost immediately became a leading scorer for Santos. By 1957 he was already on the national team. Though that year Brazil lost to Argentina in the South American championship game, Pelé scored the only goal for Brazil. Only one year later, at seventeen, he traveled to Sweden for his first World Cup match. Although he sat on the bench for most of the tournament, he played an important nonscoring role from time to time, and got his first taste of victory at its highest level when Brazil won the cup. Over the next few years, Pelé would play a growing role in World Cup competition and would be instrumental in Brazil's unprecedented third World Cup victory in 1970.

But World Cup soccer was changing from the dazzling but rather unstructured approach favored by Brazil to the disciplined, more choreographed approach favored in Europe. Additionally, in the 1970s, a more muscular and aggressive style emerged, which worked against the almost dancelike footwork of players like Pelé. Pelé retired from the national team and spent several years playing for the New York Cosmos of the North American Soccer League, which was trying to develop soccer in the United States. He then retired entirely to focus on his business ventures and educational and social opportunities he had not had as a child.

Ironically, Pelé's stature among many Brazilians dropped when he showed signs of postsoccer economic success. Apparently stories of the poor boy making good were supposed to end with a return to his original roots, and when that did not happen with Pelé, some critics called him a sellout. He lost further ground in Brazil by appearing to support the military governments and by public statements that he did not think prejudice against blacks existed in Brazil. Most Brazilians, however, admire Pelé immensely, not only for his achievements on the soccer field and in business but also for the powerful symbol of Brazilian talent and intelligence he has projected to the world. Pelé is still hugely successful as a businessman, and in 1994, a World Cup year, he matched and perhaps exceeded Michael Jordan's $30-million off-court income from endorsements.

Pelé, the renowned soccer hero and Brazilian icon, kisses the World Cup trophy won by Brazil in 1970.

"Amerindian themes, owing almost nothing to love songs . . . have brought us to a more complete lyrical contemplation of life."[23] West African influences include drumming styles, complex rhythms, and call-and-response song structures. Especially important is the influence of African dancing styles such as *umbigada,* which literally means "belly-button thrust." In all its many forms, Brazilian music is usually accompanied by sensual dancing styles rooted in African traditions. Musicologists also point to structural elements that are clearly Portuguese in origin, such as Western meters and harmonies and the syncopation that fuses so well with the African rhythms.

SAMBA

The musical form that is perceived as most essentially Brazilian is the samba. Samba has several forms, including street samba, or samba *enredo,* which predominates at Carnaval. It is characterized by loud drumming that nearly drowns out the call-and-response singing. The number of performers in a street samba can range from several dozen to several hundred. The sound of the large groups is deafening, and though nuances in the music are necessarily lost, the overall effect is electrifying.

Another form of samba is the samba *cançao,* which has the same basic samba beat but is generally a little slower and much quieter, more akin to some forms of jazz. Samba *cançao* involves smaller groups and is meant to be listened or danced to in clubs. Depending on the taste of the performers, sambas can sound fairly simple and relaxing or be more demanding due to the complexity of their rhythms. Because sambas are identified more by their rhythm than anything else, the samba is very flexible and new styles are constantly being developed.

BOSSA NOVA

In the United States the best-known Brazilian song is probably "The Girl from Ipanema," a bossa nova classic. Bossa nova is a variant of samba, but it is played on the guitar to a slowed-down, heavily syncopated beat. It arose during the 1960s out of Brazilian interest in American "cool jazz" styles and the equal interest of Americans in samba and other Brazilian musical forms. Bossa nova is difficult to play, and it

During Carnaval, hordes of costumed performers dance the samba through the streets of Brazil.

never became more than an elitist taste in Brazil. Writer Moyra Ashford quotes one guitarist as saying that bossa nova is like "talking in a long sentence, but one in which you switch language every two words."[24]

TROPICALISMO

Whereas samba is mostly for fun, Brazilian music also has a more serious side, as shown in some of the classic songs of the style known as *tropicalismo. Tropicalismo* arose in the 1960s in the state of Bahia, from which most of Brazil's great artists have come. The 1960s were a time of great change for music, emphasizing folk roots, social commentary, and electric guitars. *Tropicalismo* took a mixture of different regional musical forms from the Bahia area and incorporated elements of protest songs and electric rock into a musical form that is completely Brazilian.

HEITOR VILLA-LOBOS

Brazil's greatest classical composer, Heitor Villa-Lobos, spent his early years on Rio de Janeiro street corners and at parties and cafés playing the cello and guitar in *chôro* bands. *Chôro* is a precursor of today's samba *cançao,* focusing on highly expressive clarinet and guitar playing in small ensembles. These early experiences shaped Villa-Lobos's musical tastes and interests, and created a Brazilian sound to his classical compositions in later years. In the 1930s, Villa-Lobos, already a fairly well-known composer outside of Brazil, found himself at the center of the nationalistic enthusiasm of the Vargas years. He was put in charge of musical education in Brazil, and for the next fifteen years his efforts to promote music appreciation among children had, as a side effect, his own growing appreciation of the role Brazilian folk music could play in his own compositions.

Villa-Lobos's greatest compositions are the *Bachianas Brasileiras,* by far the most famous classical music by a Brazilian. They are the result of similarities Villa-Lobos noticed between melodies of Johann Sebastian Bach, a German composer who had died nearly two centuries earlier, and folk melodies from parts of Brazil. In the nine collections, or suites, of *Bachianas Brasileiras,* Villa-Lobos experimented with fusions of Bach and Brazilian styles, giving each piece two titles—one evoking Bach and the other a musical style of Brazil. For example, Bachianas no. 5 has two separate parts, the first titled both *aria* and *cantilena,* and the second *dansa* and *martelo. Aria* and *dansa* would have been terms familiar to Bach, and the vocal-style *cantilena* and dance-style *martelo* are familiar in Brazil. In Bachianas no. 5, an orchestra comprised only of cellos plays a melody and bass line structured like those of the baroque era in which Bach lived, but sounding rather like a plucked guitar. Soaring over this foundation is a woman's soprano voice, beautifully rising and falling in the kind of melody associated with a Brazilian love song or serenade. In the middle section the soprano sings a poem by Brazilian poet and singer Ruth Valadares Corrêa, who was the first to sing this part of Bachianas no. 5 in 1939. The second movement was added later in 1945, fusing Bach and Brazilian styles once again. This time, according to the composer, the inspiration for the melody was fragments of bird song. Villa-Lobos died in 1959.

Heitor Villa-Lobos is considered Brazil's greatest classical composer.

A giant of Brazilian music, Chico Buarque, is one of the precursors of *tropicalismo.* Buarque is known as one of the finest poets and musical figures of his time, akin perhaps to Bob Dylan or John Lennon. He started his career as a *sambista,* or samba performer. He rose to fame by writing anti-military songs, for which he was banished from Brazil for one year. He was a fine poet, adept at symbolic writing that enabled him after his return to disguise the political content of his songs and stay out of trouble with the military rulers.

Originally writing in the shadow of Buarque, Caetano Veloso emerged as one of the leaders of *tropicalismo.* He is famous both for his social criticism and his beautiful love poetry. Some of his poems have been set to music and others have been published as volumes of verse. Caetano, affectionately called by his first name by most Brazilians, is seen, according to authors David Cleary, Dilwyn Jenkins, and Oliver Marshall, as "the Leonardo da Vinci of Brazilian popular culture."[25] In addition to music and poetry, he paints, directs videos for his own songs, and is still making excellent recordings today in his early fifties.

Tropicalismo stars such as Gilberto Gil and Caetano were booed off stage at first, as was Bob Dylan in the United States when he first plugged in his electric guitar. But *tropicalismo* had tapped into a deep dissatisfaction and alienation among Brazil's youth in the 1960s, and it soon became the dominant new musical style. It also brought Afro-Brazilian pride to the surface. *Tropicalismo* superstar Gilberto Gil is black, as is Milton Nascimento, perhaps the most internationally famous. *Tropicalismo* was short-lived, but again, as with other artists in the same league, the sign of the greatness of Buarque, Caetano, Gil, and Nascimento was their ability to mature and move on to create great works in different styles. They all remain vital musical forces today.

NEW VOICES

Brazil, according to authors Cleary, Jenkins, and Marshall, is "full of people eager to argue that things aren't what they used to be."[26] Many of the liveliest discussions center around music. Some critics feel that the greatness of Brazilian music is being lost in the Westernized "global village." On the other hand, new styles are continually being produced from older, authentic Brazilian ones, and new artists such as Daniela Mercury and Margareth Menezes are quickly achieving international stardom with a distinctively Brazilian sound. They and others such as Nascimento are having their own influence on Western artists, including Paul Simon and David Byrne.

VISUAL ARTS

Brazilian art is like Brazil itself—colorful and complex. Although many contemporary artists have yet to become household names, to those in the know, they rank among the world's best.

A truly Brazilian school of artists did not emerge until the 1920s, in the aftermath of a modern art festival held in São Paulo in 1922. Earlier European traditions focused on painting

Tropicalismo *singer and musician Gilberto Gil helped bring Afro-Brazilian pride out into the open.*

what the eye perceives—either clearly, in an almost photographic manner, or distorted by things such as bright light. Modern artists such as Picasso, in contrast, commonly twisted forms into almost or completely unrecognizable shapes and reduced representations of the real world to blocks of color and shape. Picasso openly acknowledged the influence of African masks and sculptures in his art. This acknowledgment that great artistic achievement can come from non-Western styles and subject matter was instrumental in the development of new styles by non-Western artists around the world. From the 1920s on, Brazilian art has flourished by creating art that is distinctly Brazilian.

In keeping with this new Brazilian emphasis, early modern artists such as Tarsilo do Amaral coined their movement *anthropophagy,* the scientific term for "cannibalism." This term was both a bow to the practices of some Amazonian cultural groups and a way of conveying that from that point forward Brazil would feed on its own riches rather than Europe's to create art. Subject matter included African or mulatto women who conveyed physical strength as part of their overall beauty—a far cry from the pale and delicate European representations of women.

Brazilian landscapes and daily life were also depicted, perhaps most poignantly in the work of Cândido Portinari, the son of Italian immigrants who worked on the coffee plantations around São Paulo. Portinari is considered Brazil's greatest twentieth-century painter, and he tragically died from the toxins in his paints. Portinari's greatest works are his frescoes, or murals, which now are part of the United Nations building in New York and the Library of Congress in Washington, D.C. Portinari's social conscience, especially for the suffering of rural Brazilians, shows in his work. Peasants are painted with oversized hands and feet, as if to emphasize that their labor is all they possess.

Brazilian styles of painting are diverse. Artists such as Orlando Terluz, Fulvio Pennachi, and Carlos Scliar painted in realistic styles stressing Brazilian themes. Others, such as Alfred Volpi and brothers Tomas and Arcangelo Ianelli, became known for abstract, geometric styles. Some, such as Rubem Valentim, combined elements of abstract art with Brazilian symbols from Candomblé and other rituals. Others, including Mario Gruber and Ottavio Araujo, painted in a surrealist style common throughout Latin America. Their art focuses on placing recognizable objects in strange, dreamlike settings. Yet another style of painting is characterized by Nora Beltran and Gustavo Rosa. Beltran's paintings of rather silly-looking military officers and society matrons poke fun at the ruling classes, and Rosa's emphasis on the delights of daily life, such as ice cream carts and kites, focus on the lighter side of Brazilian life.

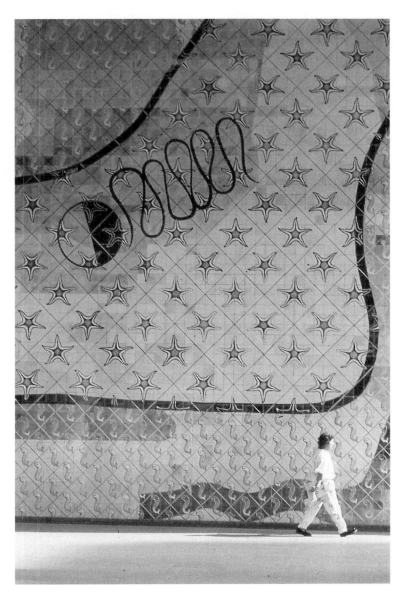

A fanciful tile artwork by Cândido Portinari graces a large wall in Rio de Janeiro.

SCULPTURE

Discussion of sculpture must begin before the modern era with the works of Aleijadinho, born Antônio Francisco Lisboa, in eighteenth-century Minas Gerais. The son of a slave woman and a Portuguese builder, he developed arthritis, which crippled his hands early in life. Undaunted, he carved by strapping implements to his wrists. In addition to designing some of the most beautiful baroque churches in Brazil, he carved dozens of soapstone and wood statues, including sixty-six figures representing the Catholic Stations of the Cross, which are considered his masterpiece. Aleijadinho never went to school and never even saw the ocean, yet he created one of the greatest art legacies in Brazil, and his genius and unquenchable desire to create have made him one of the most inspirational figures in Brazilian arts.

Aleijadinho's subject matter came from his Catholic faith. Another spiritual foundation for much of Brazilian sculpture comes from more ancient folk traditions. Among these, the legends associated with the São Francisco River in central Brazil are most prominent. Old Chico, as the São Francisco is commonly known, is thought to be the home of many evil spirits. Beginning in the nineteenth century, people along the river began carving ugly half-man, half-animal figureheads called *carrancas* for their boats. Traditionally, these statues would be positioned on the front of the boats so that they would look down into the water and scare off the bad spirits. The *carrancas* were also believed to moan if the boat was in danger. Today few people of the São Francisco riverbanks believe in the *carrancas,* but the idea that carvings can exude great spiritual force has exerted a great influence on contemporary sculptors. For example, renowned sculptor Maurino Araujo combines the influences of the *carrancas* and Aleijadinho in his art, creating wood carvings of deformed and rather macabre angels.

Modern sculptures are everywhere in urban Brazil, many of them by second-generation Brazilians or immigrants of Italian or Japanese descent. Examples include Ceschiatti's bronze of two women combing their hair, which is displayed in a pool on the grounds of the president's palace in Brasília, and his mobile of angels in the cathedral of Brasília. A Japanese immigrant named Toyota has received acclaim

THE SÃO PAULO BIENAL

Ibirapuera, a large park in downtown São Paulo, houses a three-story pavilion constructed primarily of ramps and glass that houses the São Paulo Bienal. The Bienal is the largest regularly scheduled art event in the world. Only a similar show in Venice is equally important. The Bienal has been held every two years since 1951 and lasts several months. Participating countries send works by the artists they consider most important and influential, and the Bienal curators select a few themselves to showcase. Those artists selected by the curators can be living or dead, but the other entries must be works by living artists. The emphasis, therefore, has come to be on innovative new artists and retrospectives of established first-rate ones. Critics argue that much of the art seems to focus more on being original than on being good, and in some years the Bienal has not gotten good reviews, although in others it has lived up to its reputation to identify and showcase great artists on the cutting edge.

São Paulo has a long history of interest in the arts. It was a show held in this city that inspired Brazilian artists to break with European traditions in the 1920s. Connected to the Bienal Pavilion is the Museum of Modern Art, which houses a fine collection of works by Brazil's contemporary painters and sculptors, the current generation of artists benefiting from the visions of those who went before them.

The modern Bienal Pavilion hosts the São Paulo Bienal, the world's largest international art event.

for his mobiles and sculptures, including one made of polished steel rods resembling a chandelier that is displayed outside a hotel in São Paulo. Dominique Calabrone creates large stone and metal sculptures for public places, and Franco de Renzis creates works that feature horses or human figures arranged in gravity defying positions.

In a related but completely different art form, Brazil is acclaimed for its modern tapestries. Madeleine and Concessa Colaco, a Tangiers-born mother and daughter team, use a new process called the Brazilian stitch, which Madeleine invented. Jacques Douchez and Norberto Nicola have taken tapestry in a new direction by incorporating rope and plant fibers in their abstract designs.

ARCHITECTURE

The capital city of Brasília is a showcase for the genius of modern Brazilian architects. In fact, the seeds were planted for Brazil's move to the forefront of architecture several decades earlier when, in 1930, the great French architect Le Corbusier was invited to give a lecture series in Brazil. Le Corbusier's approach was perfect for the tropical climate of Brazil, focusing on open spaces, large windows, patios, and simple lines. Le Corbusier's ideas were implemented by a Brazilian team, including urban planner Lucio Costa, landscape architect Roberto Burle-Marx, and architect Oscar Niemeyer, who together designed the education ministry building in Rio de Janeiro. This team was reunited by Juscelino Kubitschek when he was mayor of Belo Horizonte to build what is considered the most pleasant urban park in Brazil, Pampulha. According to author Tom Murphy, "The overall effect is an architecture of fresh, light structures which seem to hover over the green parkland and the blue waters of the artificial Lake Pampulha."[27] Kubitschek called the same group of architects together again when plans to build a new capital city, Brasília, were laid. The result is still considered a marvel of city planning and engineering unequaled anywhere in the world.

LITERATURE

Brazil has produced several of the most important writers of modern times. Among them is Jorge Amado, a Bahian. His works have been translated into over forty languages and

The Brasília National Cathedral, designed by prominent architect Oscar Niemeyer, is one of many architectural treasures found in Brazil's capital.

several have been made into films, including his novels *Gabriela* and *Dona Flor and Her Two Husbands.* One of his most acclaimed works is *Tent of Miracles,* a novel about an Afro-Brazilian who fights prejudice in 1930s Brazil.

Another well-known Brazilian novelist is Mário de Andrade. His 1928 novel *Macunaíma* is the story of a folk hero from the jungle interior of Brazil, and it is considered by many to be the greatest single work of Brazilian literature. Others, however, think Brazil's greatest fiction writer is Joaquim Machado de Assis, whose black humor and cool wit make *The Devil's Church* and *Helena* wonderful reading. Another popular Brazilian writer is João Ubaldo Ribeiro, whose epic *An Invincible Memory* is the saga of two Bahia families, one white, one black, from colonial times to the present.

BUMBA-MEU-BOI

According to writer David Cleary in *Brazil: The Rough Guide,* "There's no more atmospheric popular festival in Brazil" than Bumba-meu-boi. This is quite a statement for the country that created Carnaval, but those people who make the annual June trip to Bumba-meu-boi would no doubt agree.

The festival takes place in San Luis, the capital city of the state of Maranhão. Bumba-meu-boi is a dance, performed by troupes of costumed characters who act out the story of a plantation owner who leaves a bull in the care of a slave. The bull dies, but is magically brought back to life, and the slave avoids punishment. In the reenactment, the bull costume is fashioned out of black velvet trimmed with sequins. The person inside the costume whirls around, surrounded by musicians. The songs are first sung by a single person to the accompaniment of a mandolin. Then, because the songs are familiar, when the brass instruments and drums come in, everyone bursts into song, accompanied by dancers. David Cleary elaborates on the festival:

> You couldn't wish for a clearer symbol of the cultural influences that make Brazil what it is: the brass sounds Mediterranean, the dancers dress as Indians, and the drumming is like nothing you'll have ever heard. Bumba drums are unique: hollow, and played by strumming a metal spring inside, they give out a deep, haunting, hypnotically powerful backbeat.

At the end of the performance, near dawn, the strains of the city's unofficial anthem are heard, and everyone joins in singing loudly. The sound can be heard over much of San Luis.

Although not a fiction writer, one of the most influential writers in twentieth-century Brazil is Gilberto Freyre, who wrote histories and sociological analyses of Brazilian culture in the 1930s. His most famous work is *The Masters and the Slaves,* in which he puts forth the now widely rejected point of view that Brazil is a racial democracy, immune to racism. Another well-known book by Freyre is *The Mansions and the Shanties,* about the early history and growth of the cities of Brazil.

In the twentieth century, Brazil has taken its place as one of the world's great centers of visual, literary, and musical arts. No doubt this is at least part of the reason why, despite all the difficulties of daily life for many Brazilians, a recent poll indicated that the overwhelming majority would not consider living anywhere else. Between the excitement of *futebol* and the *telenovelas,* the lively nightlife of both cities and smaller towns, and the stunning achievements in all the arts, Brazilians today live in the middle of a kaleidoscope of colors, sounds, and artistic creations that are an essential part of national pride.

FACTS ABOUT BRAZIL

GOVERNMENT

Official name: Federative Republic of Brazil (República Federativa do Brasil)

Capital: Brasília, in the Federal District of Brasília

Political subdivisions: 26 states and 1 federal district

Type of government: Federal republic headed by a president

Current number of political parties: 14

Independence date: September 7, 1822

Total membership in national congress: Chamber of Deputies, 513; Federal Senate, 81

PEOPLE

Total population: 160 million (1998 estimate)

Population growth rate: 1.24%

Life expectancy: At birth, 64.36 years; male, 59.39 years; female, 69.59 years; infant deaths per 1,000 live births, 36.96

Ethnicity: white, 55%; mixed white/black, 38%; black, 6%; other (Asian, Arab, Indian), 1%

Literacy rate (for Brazilians over age 15): 83.3%

Religion: Roman Catholic, 70%; Protestant, 19%; other, 11%

GEOGRAPHY

Area: 5,319,978 square miles (8,511,965 square kilometers)

Coastline: 4,682 miles (7,491 kilometers)

Climate: Mostly tropical but temperate in far south

Land use: Arable land, 5%; permanent cropland, 1%; permanent pastures, 22%; forests and woodlands, 58%; other, 14%

Borders: French Guyana, Suriname, Guyana, Venezuela, Colombia, Peru, Bolivia, Paraguay, Argentina, Uruguay (all South American countries except Chile and Ecuador)

ECONOMY

Monetary unit (since 1994): real

Previous monetary units: cruzeiro, cruzado

Labor force: 66.9 million employees, ten years of age or older (1994 estimate); agricultural/forestry/fishing, 29.2%; trade/financial services, 21.7%; manufacturing, 16%; retail/restaurants/hotels, 9.3%; construction, 7.4%; transportation/communications, 4.2%; other, 2%; unemployed, 2.3%

Annual inflation rate: 1989, 1,320%; 1990, 2,739.7%; 1991, 414.7%; 1992, 991.4%; 1993, 2,103.7%; 1994, 2,406.8%; 1995, 14.8%; 1996, 9.5%

Average annual per capita income: $4,086 (1995 estimate)

Those classified as living in extreme poverty: 32 million

    percentage of those living in metropolitan areas: 9.6%

    percentage of those living in other urban areas: 18.4%

    percentage of those living in rural areas: 42.8%

Natural resources: Bauxite, gold, iron ore, manganese, nickel, phosphates, platinum, tin, uranium, petroleum, hydropower, timber

Exports: $49.2 billion (1997 estimate); tin, iron, manganese, steel, sugar, coffee, soybeans, orange juice

Major export markets: United States, Argentina, Japan, Netherlands

NOTES

CHAPTER 1: ALMOST A CONTINENT: THE LAND

1. Quoted in Edwin Taylor, ed., *Insight Guides: Brazil.* Singapore: APA, 1998, p. 274.

CHAPTER 2: THE COLONY OF BRAZIL

2. John A. Crow, *The Epic of Latin America.* 4th ed. Berkeley and Los Angeles: University of California Press, 1992, p. 138.

3. Pamela Bloom, *Brazil.* Redondo Beach, CA: Fielding Worldwide, 1994, p. 39.

4. David Cleary, Dilwyn Jenkins, and Oliver Marshall, *Brazil: The Rough Guide.* London: Rough Guides, 1998, p. 603.

5. Cleary, Jenkins, and Marshall, *Brazil,* p. 603.

CHAPTER 3: THE NINETEENTH-CENTURY EMPIRE OF BRAZIL

6. Crow, *The Epic of Latin America,* p. 521.

7. Crow, *The Epic of Latin America,* p. 526.

8. Taylor, *Insight Guides,* p. 38.

9. Crow, *The Epic of Latin America,* p. 557.

CHAPTER 4: THE REPUBLIC OF BRAZIL

10. Taylor, *Insight Guides,* p. 39.

11. Cleary, Jenkins, and Marshall, *Brazil,* p. 612.

12. Cleary, Jenkins, and Marshall, *Brazil,* p. 613.

CHAPTER 5: LAND OF MANY COLORS: THE PEOPLE OF BRAZIL

13. Joseph A. Page, *The Brazilians.* Reading, MA: Addison-Wesley, 1995, p. 85.

14. Page, *The Brazilians,* p. 90.

15. Quoted in Page, *The Brazilians,* p. 89.

16. Page, *The Brazilians,* p. 354.

17. Page, *The Brazilians,* p. 364.

18. Quoted in Taylor, *Insight Guides,* p. 67.

CHAPTER 6: THE CHALLENGES OF CONTEMPORARY BRAZIL

19. Quoted in Page, *The Brazilians,* p. 193.

20. Page, *The Brazilians,* p. 195.

21. Quoted in Page, *The Brazilians,* p. 317.

22. Quoted in Page, *The Brazilians,* p. 287.

CHAPTER 7: ARTS AND ENTERTAINMENT IN THE LAND OF CARNAVAL

23. Quoted in Taylor, *Insight Guides,* p. 114.

24. Quoted in Taylor, *Insight Guides,* p. 118.

25. Cleary, Jenkins, and Marshall, *Brazil,* p. 566.

26. Cleary, Jenkins, and Marshall, *Brazil,* p. 567.

27. Quoted in Taylor, *Insight Guides,* p. 133.

GLOSSARY

bandeirante: Brazilian term for an explorer of the interior of Brazil.

call-and-response: A song style characterized by one person singing a line, followed by a chorus repeating either that line or a response to that line.

favela: Brazilian term for slum.

indigenous: Native to the area.

jeito: Brazilian term for a creative solution or quick fix.

mameluco: Brazilian term for a person of mixed Portuguese and Indian ancestry.

mulatto: A person of mixed African and white ancestry.

musicologist: A person who studies music.

orixá: An African word for a god or goddess.

polyrhythm: A form of music in which several different rhythms are played at the same time.

regency: A period of time when the rightful king or queen is either too young or otherwise unable to rule and others rule in his or her place.

sertão: Brazilian term for the dry, hot interior of the northeast.

syncretism: The process by which cultures borrow from each other and develop new art forms.

CHRONOLOGY

1494
Treaty of Tordesillas divides New World between Portugal and Spain.

1500
Pedro Álvars Cabral lands on coast of Brazil.

1532
Sugarcane is first grown in Brazil.

1549
Salvador becomes capital of Brazil.

1630
The Dutch invade Brazil.

1654
The Dutch are pushed out of Brazil.

1698
Gold is found in Minas Gerais.

1725
Gold is found in Goiás.

1729
Diamonds are found in Minas Gerais.

1763
Capital is moved to Rio de Janeiro.

1808
Portuguese royal court moves to Rio de Janeiro.

1816
Dom João becomes King John VI of Portugal and Brazil.

1821
King John VI returns to Portugal; names son Pedro as regent in Brazil.

1822
Brazil declares independence; Dom Pedro becomes
Emperor Pedro I.

1831
Pedro I abdicates throne; Pedro II becomes monarch;
regents rule Brazil.

1841
Pedro takes throne as Pedro II.

1888
Slavery is abolished in Brazil.

1889
Pedro is overthrown; Brazil declares itself a republic.

1891
First constitution is approved.

1917
Brazil enters World War I on side of Allies.

1930
Getúlio Vargas overthrows government.

1934
Second constitution is adopted; Vargas is elected president.

1937
Vargas establishes "New State;" becomes dictator.

1945
Coup removes Vargas from office.

1946
New constitution is adopted.

1950
Vargas is once again elected president.

1954
Vargas is forced to resign.

1956
Juscelino Kubitschek is elected president.

1960
Brasília becomes new capital of Brazil.

1964
Coup results in military-backed government.

1967
Fifth constitution is adopted.

1969
Emilio Medici becomes president.

1974
Ernesto Geisel becomes president.

1978
João Figueiredo is elected president; political reforms begin.

1985
Military steps down from power; democracy is restored; Tancredo Neves is elected president; José Sarney is inaugurated after Neves's death.

1990
Fernando Collor de Mello is elected president.

1992
President Collor is impeached.

1994
New currency, the real, is introduced, tied to Plano Real.

1995
Fernando Henrique Cardoso is inaugurated as president.

1998
Cardoso is reelected.

SUGGESTIONS FOR FURTHER READING

Books

Bira Almeida, *Capoeira: A Brazilian Art Form.* Berkeley, CA: North Atlantic Books, 1986. A thorough discussion of *capoeira* by a noted master, including information about its history, its music, and its moves.

E. Bradford Burns, *History of Brazil.* New York: Columbia University Press, 1993. Acclaimed study of Brazil, including analysis of contemporary issues and trends.

Wilbur and Susanna Cross, *Brazil.* Chicago: Childrens Press, 1984. Easy-to-read book, full of good general information and pictures.

Marshall C. Eakin, *Brazil: The Once and Future Country.* New York: St. Martin's, 1997. Authoritative survey of historical and contemporary Brazil.

Annette Haddad and Scott Doggett, eds., *Travelers' Tales: Brazil.* San Francisco: Travelers' Tales, 1997. Essays by different authors about their experiences in Brazil.

Claude Levi-Strauss, *Tristes Tropiques.* New York: Penguin, 1992. This famous work by a prominent anthropologist, first published in 1955, is still considered the classic study of the indigenous groups of the Amazon.

Chris McGowan and Ricardo Pessanha, *The Brazilian Sound: Samba, Bossa Nova, and the Popular Music of Brazil.* Philadelphia: Temple University Press, 1998. Lots of pictures and a good introduction to the music of Brazil.

National Geographic Society, *Exploring the Amazon.* Washington, DC: National Geographic Society, 1970. Excellent photographs accompanying a travel narrative.

117

Geoffrey O'Connor, *Dispatches from a Vanishing Frontier.* New York: Plume, 1998. Noted documentary filmmaker combines photographs and personal memoirs with history and anthropology to create a powerful study of the struggles over the future of the Amazon.

Sebastiao Salgado, *Terra: Struggle of the Landless.* London: Phaidon, 1997. Acclaimed black-and-white photo essay concerning the plight of the rural poor.

Websites

Amazonian (www.amazonian.org). Website of a nonprofit organization involved with environmental projects in the Amazon basin.

Brazil.com (www.brazil-brasil.com). This site is a clearing house for information and links to information about contemporary Brazil. Link to *Brazzil,* an on-line magazine mostly in English (Rodney Mello, editor).

Brazilonline (www.brazilonline.com). This site, edited by Guilherme Verguiero, contains articles on Brazilian history, art, culture, and politics.

Greenpeace (www.greenpeace.org). Information on the Amazon and other areas by the world's leading environmental advocates.

Maria-Brazil (www.maria-brazil.org). A fun site focusing on photos, recipes, stories, and other subjects by editors who clearly love Brazil.

WORKS CONSULTED

Books

Peter Bakewell, *A History of Latin America.* Malden, MA: Blackwell, 1997. A complete history of Latin America with a good section on the economic and social structure of colonial Brazil.

Pamela Bloom, *Brazil.* Redondo Beach, CA: Fielding World-wide, 1994. Provides good historical and cultural information on Brazil.

David Cleary, Dilwyn Jenkins, and Oliver Marshall, *Brazil: The Rough Guide.* London: Rough Guides, 1998. Excellent source of detailed information about interesting people, places, and events often overlooked by other guides. Very thorough geographic information, designed for tourists.

John A. Crow, *The Epic of Latin America.* 4th ed. Berkeley and Los Angeles: University of California Press, 1992. Many chapters on Brazilian history, from early European contact to the 1990s, although contemporary information is not as extensive.

Editors of Time-Life Books, *Brazil.* Alexandria, VA: Time-Life Books, 1988. A good abbreviated history of Brazil, coupled with interesting photo essays about aspects of Brazilian life and other information.

Rex A. Hudson, ed., *Brazil: A Country Study.* 5th ed. Washington, DC: Library of Congress, Federal Research Division, 1998. One volume in a series sponsored by the U.S. Army, presenting up-to-date information about Brazil's economy, politics, history, and people.

Joseph A. Page, *The Brazilians.* Reading, MA: Addison-Wesley, 1995. Good portrait of modern Brazil, focusing on the characteristics and lifestyles of its inhabitants.

J. H. Parry, *The Discovery of South America*. New York: Taplinger, 1979. Tells the story of early Portuguese contacts in Brazil, largely through letters, journals, and other documents.

Anthony Smith, *Explorers of the Amazon*. London: Viking, 1990. Interesting and detailed information about the men and women who explored the Amazon Basin from the time of Cabral through the rubber boom.

Edwin Taylor, ed., *Insight Guides: Brazil*. Singapore: APA, 1998. Excellent photographs and essays on various aspects of life in Brazil, geographical regions, and history.

Periodicals

Robert Laxalt, "Gauchos: Last of a Breed," *National Geographic*, October 1980.

INDEX

Acre, 11, 88
Africans
 music of, 69–70
 as plantation slaves, 28–29
 religious cults of, 70, 72–74
Aleijadinho, 102
Alvarez, Diogo, 26
Amado, Jorge, 104–105
Amaral, Crispin do, 56
Amaral, Tarsilo do, 100
Amazon rain forest
 destruction of, 87, 89
Amazon River, 10–11
American Revolution, 34
Andrade, Mário de, 93, 95,
 105
Angelim, Eduardo, 45
anthropophagy, 100
Araguaia River, 19
Araujo, Maurino, 102
Araujo, Ottavio, 100–101
architecture, 14, 104
Argentina, 47
art, visual, 99–101, 103
Assis, Joaquim Machado de,
 105

Bahia, 12–13, 14, 71
Balbina, 89
bandeirantes (colonists),
 29–30
 gold mining and, 31, 33
Belém, 11, 45
Belo Horizonte, 17–18
Beltran, Nora, 101
Bienal Pavilion, 103
Bloom, Pamela, 30
Bolívar, Simon, 43–44

Bonaparte, Napoléon, 37
Bonifácio de Andrada e Silva,
 José, 41
 dismissal of, 43
 role in Brazilian history, 42
bossa nova, 95–96
Brasília, 20, 104
 building of, 58, 61
Brasília Teimosa, 85
Brazil
 architecture of, 14, 104
 Constitution of, 51
 crime/violence in, 83–84, 87
 during regency period,
 44–46
 economy, 63–64
 class inequalities and,
 81–83
 development of, 53–55
 environmental/social problems, 6–8, 87, 89
 ethnic diversity in, 9, 65
 interracial relationships
 and, 28–29
 racism and, 76, 78–79
 geography of, 10
 Center-West, 18–20
 Northeastern, 12–15
 Northern, 10–12
 Southeastern, 15–18
 Southern, 20–21
 gold rush in, 31, 33–35
 identity of people in, 3, 39,
 41
 immigrants to, 76
 independence of, 34, 41–44
 literature of, 104–106
 living for oneself in, 6–8, 80

121

music of, 93, 95–99
pollution in, 90–92
Portuguese colonization of, 23–27
Portuguese court moved to, 37–39
presidents of, 51–53, 58–60, 63–64
racism in, 76, 78–79
reforms in, 57
relations with Portuguese, 36, 37
sculpture of, 102, 104
under Cardoso, 63–64
visual arts in, 99–101, 103
brazilwood, 24, 25
British, 45
Buarque, Chico, 98
Bumba-meu-boi, 106
Burle-Marx, Roberto, 104
Byrne, David, 99

Cabanagem Rebellion, 44, 45
Cabral, Pedro Álvars, 23–24
Calabrone, Dominique, 104
Candelaria Massacre, 86
Candomblé (religious cult), 70, 72
cannibalism, 24, 26
Canudos, 53
Capela Dourada, 14
capoeira, 14
captaincies, system of, 27
Caramaru, 26
Cardoso, Fernando Henrique, 9, 80–81
  on agrarian reform, 84
  reform under, 63–64
Carlota, Queen of Portugal, 40
Carnaval, 8, 15–16, 71
Carreras, José, 56
Caruso, Enrico, 56
Catholicism, 74
  see also missionaries
cattle ranching, 35–36, 88, 89

Ceschiatti, 102
Chaves, Nelson, 83
children
  execution of, 86
  poverty of, 80
chôro bands, 97
Christianity, 25, 74
churches, 17
classical music, 97
Cleary, David, 13, 30, 60, 98, 106
coffee, 53–54
Colaco, Concessa, 104
Colaco, Madeleine, 104
colonists, 24–27
  relations with Indians, 66–67
  relations with slaves, 69
  see also bandeirantes
Confederacy of Plamares, 31
Conselheiro, Antonio, 53
Constitution
  Brazilian, 51
  U.S., 34
Corrêa, Ruth Valadares, 97
Costa, Lucio, 61, 104
crime, 83–84, 87
  death squads and, 86
  poverty and, 81
Cristina, Tereza (Empress)
  city named after, 16
Crow, John A., 25, 38, 40, 42, 50
Cubatão, 91
Cuiabá, 19–20, 33
cults, religious, 70, 72–74

dance, 95, 106
death squads, 83, 86
degradados (criminals), 24–25
Devil's Church, The (Machado de Assis), 105
Diamantina, 18, 33
diamond mining, 33
Dona Flor and Her Two Husbands (Amado), 105

Douchez, Jacques, 104
Dutch, 25–26

economy, 58–59
  inequalities of wealth and,
    8, 81–83
  natural resources and,
    53–55
  revitalization of, 63–64
education, 48–49
elections, 59, 60, 62
ethnic diversity, 9, 65
  racism and, 76, 78–79

faith healing, 66–67
Farraoupilha (Ragamuffins)
  Rebellion, 44
favela, 85
  crime by, 80, 83
  pollution and, 91
Fonseca, Manuel Deodoro
  da, 49, 51–52
French, 25–26
Freyre, Gilberto, 106

Gabriela (Amado), 105
Gama, Vasco da, 23
Germans, 76, 77
Gilberto, Gil, 98
Goiás, 20, 33
Golden Chapel, 14
Golden Law, 47–48
gold mining, 31, 33, 35
gold rush, 31, 33
  influence of, 35–36
Goodyear, Charles, 55
Gruber, Mario, 100–101
Guanabara Bay, 90

Helena (Machado de Assis),
  105
Herrington, Elizabeth, 15
hot springs, 20
House, Richard, 15
hygiene, 67–68

Ianelli, Arcangelo, 100
Ianelli, Tomas, 100
Ibirapuera Park, 103
Iemanjá, 73
Iguazú Falls, 21
Inconfidencia Mineira, 34
Indians
  on brazilwood, 25
  characteristics of, 66–69
  influence in music, 93, 95
  Jesuit protection of, 32
  park for, 19
  as plantation slaves, 28
  Portuguese and, 23, 24, 26
interracial relationships,
  28–29
Invincible Memory, An
  (Ribeiro), 105
Isabel, Princess of Brazil,
  47–48
Itaimbezinho Canyon, 21
Itaipú hydroelectric plant, 21

Japanese, 78
Jefferson, Thomas, 34
Jenkins, Dilwyn, 30, 60, 98
Jesuit missionaries, 25, 32
  on slavery, 28
João, Regent Dom, 37–38
  reforms under, 38–39
  return to Portugal, 39–40, 41
Jogo do Bicho ("Game of the
  Animals"), 66–67
John VI, King of Portugal, 39

Kardec, Alain, 72–73
Kubitschek, Juscelino, 58–59
  birthplace of, 18
  Brasília and, 20, 61

land disputes, 84
language, 74–75, 77
Le Corbusier (French architect), 104
Liberdade, 78

Lincoln, Abraham, 46
Lisboa, Antônio Francisco, 102
literature, 104–106
logging, 6–7
Lula, 62

Macunaíma (de Andrade), 105
mamelucos, 26, 28, 36
Manaus, 11–12, 55, 56
Mansions and the Shanties, The (Freyre), 106
Manuel I, King of Portugal, 23
Maria, Queen of Portugal, 37, 40
Marshall, Oliver, 30, 60, 98
Masters and the Slaves, The (Freyre), 106
Mato Grosso, 19–20
Mato Grosso do Sul, 19–20
Mello, Fernando Collor de, 60, 62, 63
Mendes, Chico, 87, 88
Menezes, Margaret, 98–99
Mercury, Daniela, 98–99
military, 47
  political influence of, 52–53, 59
  revolts by, 57
  role of, 51
Minas Conspiracy, 34
Minas Gerais, 17–18, 31
mining
  failure of, 6–7
  gold/diamond, 17, 31, 33, 35
missionaries, 25, 28, 32
Morais Barros, Prudent José de, 53
Murphy, Tom, 76, 104
music, 93, 98–99
  bossa nova, 95–96
  classical, 97
  samba, 69–70, 71, 95
  tropicalismo, 96, 98

Nascimento, Edson Arantes do, 94
Nascimento, Milton, 98
natural resources
  brazilwood, 24, 25
  diamonds/gold, 31, 33–35
  vs. living for today, 6–8
  rubber, 54–55
Neiva, Tia, 74
New Christians (recently converted Jews), 24
Nicola, Norberto, 104
Niemeyer, Oscar, 61, 104
Nossa Senhora do Pilar (church), 17

Old Chico (São Francisco River), 102
Olinda, 14
orixás (gods and goddesses), 70, 73
Ouro Prêto, 17

Page, Joseph A., 66, 70, 91
Pampulha, 104
Pantanal, 18–19
Paraguay, 47
Paraná, 20–21
parks, 19, 20–21
patrias (regional governments), 44
Pedro I, 41–42
  city named after, 16
  leadership of, 43–44
Pedro II, 41–42
  city named after, 16
  fall of, 49–50
  reign of, 46–49
Peixoto, Floriano, 51, 52
Pelé, 93, 94
Pennachi, Fulvio, 100
Pernambuco, 12–13, 31
Petrópolis, 16
Picasso, 100
Plano Real, 63

police corruption, 84, 86
pollution, 90–92
Portinari, Cândido, 100
Pôrto Alegre, 21
Pôrto Velho, 11
Portugal
  and Brazilian development, 33, 35
  Brazilian perception of, 39
  colonization by, 23–27
  influence on Brazil, 74–75
  relations with Brazil, 36, 37
  relocation of court, 37–39, 40
  taxes by, 34
  see also colonists
Portuguese
  arrival of in Brazil, 23–24
  colonization by, 24–27
  influence of, 74–75
poverty, 81–83

quilombos (forest communities), 31

racism, 76, 78–79
rain forest, destruction of, 87, 89
Ramalho, João, 26
rebellions, 44, 45, 57
Recife, 14, 85
Rei Momo, 71
religious cults, 70, 72–74
Renzis, Franco de, 104
Ribeiro, João Ubaldo, 105
Rio de Janeiro, 8, 15–16
  founding of, 27
  gold rush and, 35
  Portuguese court moved to, 37–39
Rio Grande do Norte, 12–13
Rio Grande do Sul, 21
Rocinha, 81–82
Rondon, Cândido, 13
Rondônia, 11, 13

Rosa, Gustavo, 101
Rosas, Juan Manual de, 47
rubber, 54–55, 88

Salvador, 14, 27
samba, 69–70, 95
  in Carnaval, 71
San Luis, 106
Santa Catarina, 21, 77
Santos, 27
São Francisco River, 102
São Paulo, 6, 17, 27
  arts event in, 103
  gold rush and, 35
  Japanese in, 78
  pollution in, 90, 92
São Paulo Bienal, 103
Sarney, José, 60
Scliar, Carlos, 100
sculpture, 102, 104
sertão (inland region), 13, 14–15
  poverty in, 83
Service for the Protection of the Indians (SPI), 13
Silva, Luis Inacio da, 62
Silva Xavier, Joaquim José da, 34
Simon, Paul, 99
slavery, 28–29
  abolishment of, 47–48
  disagreements on, 44
  opposition to, 32
slaves, African
  confederacy of, 31
  cults of, 70, 72–74
  music of, 69–70
soccer, 93, 94
Sousa, Martim Afonso de, 26, 27
Sousa, Tomé de, 27
Spain, 23
sugar
  demand for, 27–28
  plantations for, 28–29

syncretism, 65

Taylor, Edwin, 43, 52–53
Teatro Amazonas, 56
telenovelas, 93
Teresópolis, 16
Terluz, Orlando, 100
Terra do Brasil, 24
Tiradentes, 34
Toyota, 102, 104
Trans-Amazon Highway, 11,
   88
tropicalismo, 96, 98
Tucuruí, 89

Umbanda, 72–74
umbigada (dancing styles), 95
Uruguay, 43, 47

Vale do Amanhecer, 74
Valentim, Rubem, 100
Valley of Dawn, 74
Vargas, Getúlio, 55, 57–58
Velhos, Domingos Jorge, 31

Veloso, Caetano, 98
Venezuela, 43–44
Vieira, Antonio, 32
Vila Velha State Park, 20–21
Villa-Lobos, Heitor, 97
visual arts, 99–100, 103
Volpi, Alfred, 100
voting, 48

war
   civil, 52, 53
   with Paraguay, 47
War of the Triple Alliance, 47
waterfalls, 21
women, 28–29
Workers' Party (PT), 62
World War II, 58, 77

Xingú National Park, 19

Yanomami, 6
   see also Indians
Yanomami Indigenous Park,
   19

PICTURE CREDITS

Cover photo: © Eduardo Garcia/FPG International
Vanderlei Almeida/Reuters/Archive Photos, 64
AP/Wide World Photos, 58, 59
Archive Photos, 16, 46, 73, 82, 96
Corbis, 24, 48
Corbis/AFP, 99
Corbis/Barnabas Bosshart, 86
Corbis/Joel Creed; Ecoscene, 11
Corbis/Ed Eckstein, 85
Corbis/Arne Hodalic, 25
Corbis/Jeremy Horner, 81
Corbis/Stephanie Maze, 35, 77, 103
Corbis/Francesco Venturi; Kea Publishing Services Ltd., 40
Corbis-Bettmann, 29, 41, 52, 61, 97
Corbis-Bettmann/UPI, 49
Digital Vision, 68, 91
FPG International, 22, 54, 67
Imapress/Archive Photos, 71
© Don Klein, 8 (both), 9, 15, 18, 21, 56, 66, 72, 75, 101, 105
Library of Congress, 38
Lineworks, Incorporated, 7, 90
North Wind Picture Archives, 31, 32, 50
Popperfoto/Archive Photos, 94
Reuters/Agencia Estado/Archive Photos, 88
Reuters/Mark Cardwell/Archive Photos, 62

ABOUT THE AUTHOR

Laurel Corona lives in Lake Arrowhead, California, and teaches English and humanities at San Diego City College. She has a master's degree from the University of Chicago and a Ph.D. from the University of California at Davis.